SOCIAL MEDIA IN ACADEMIA

Social media and online social networks are expected to transform academia and the scholarly process. However, intense emotions permeate scholars' online practices and an increasing number of academics are finding themselves in trouble in networked spaces. In reality, the evidence describing scholars' experiences in online social networks and social media is fragmented. As a result, the ways that social media are used and experienced by scholars are not well understood. *Social Media in Academia* examines the day-to-day realities of social media and online networks for scholarship and illuminates the opportunities, tensions, conflicts, and inequities that exist in these spaces. The book concludes with suggestions for institutions, individual scholars, and doctoral students regarding online participation, social media, networked practice, and public scholarship.

George Veletsianos is Canada Research Chair of Innovative Learning and Technology and Associate Professor at Royal Roads University in Victoria, British Columbia, Canada. He has been developing and researching digital learning environments since 2004.

SOCIAL MEDIA IN ACADEMIA

Networked Scholars

George Veletsianos

Routledge
Taylor & Francis Group

NEW YORK AND LONDON

First published 2016
by Routledge
711 Third Avenue, New York, NY 10017

and by Routledge
2 Park Square, Milton Park, Abingdon, Oxon OX14 4RN

Routledge is an imprint of the Taylor & Francis Group, an informa business

© 2016 Taylor & Francis

The right of George Veletsianos to be identified as the author of this work
has been asserted by him in accordance with sections 77 and 78 of the
Copyright, Designs and Patents Act 1988.

Library of Congress Cataloging in Publication Data
Names: Veletsianos, George.
Title: Social media in academia : networked scholars / George Veletsianos.
Description: New York, NY : Routledge, 2016. | Includes bibliographical
references and index.
Identifiers: LCCN 2015025278| ISBN 9781138822740 (hardback) | ISBN
9781138822757 (pbk.) | ISBN 9781315742298 (ebook)
Subjects: LCSH: Communication in education. | Learning and
scholarship--Technological innovations. | Social media. | Online social
networks.
Classification: LCC LB1033.5 .V45 2016 | DDC 378.1/98--dc23
LC record available at http://lccn.loc.gov/2015025278

ISBN: 978-1-138-82274-0 (hbk)
ISBN: 978-1-138-82275-7 (pbk)
ISBN: 978-1-315-74229-8 (ebk)

Typeset in Bembo
by Saxon Graphics Ltd, Derby

For Stella and Nicos.
And Magda and Nicoletta.
And Kelly.

CONTENTS

ACKNOWLEDGEMENTS

This book has been in development for many years. It draws on studies that were conducted as early as 2009 and it owes its existence to research I have conducted with Royce Kimmons. I met Royce when he was a PhD student at the University of Texas at Austin. I interviewed for a position there in 2009 and as part of the interview process I had lunch with MA and PhD students. Royce asked me about my research interests. I asked him about his. That was the first of many interactions, and I eventually have had the distinct pleasure and privilege of being the chair of his dissertation committee. Royce and I conducted research on networked participatory scholarship and social networking sites while we were at the University of Texas at Austin, and have continued this collaboration since then, even though I have moved to Royal Roads University and he has moved to the University of Idaho and then Brigham Young University. My collaboration with Royce has been one of the most exciting and engaging of my career – Royce's insights and knowledge have a lot to do with that.

Throughout my career, I have had the fortune to interact with a network of peers and colleagues who have helped me make better sense of networked scholarship. Without them this book would not have happened. These colleagues have helped me by publishing their own writing on the topic, by critiquing early drafts of my work, by commenting on my work, by writing with me, and by interacting with me in conferences, symposia, and telephone calls. They've also helped me by just being themselves, by being amazing scholars who do creative and important scholarship.

This global network of peers includes Joan Hughes, Martin Weller, Audrey Watters, Richard Hall, Amy Collier, Drew Whitworth, George Siemens, Bonnie Stewart, Curt Bonk, Kate Bowles, Anatoliy Gruzd, Cassie Scharber, Andy Gibbons, Christine Greenhow, Alec Couros, Tom Reeves, Terry Anderson,

Laura Czerniewicz, Sian Bayne, Jen Ross, Ana-Paula Correia, Patrick Lowenthal, Clint Lalonde, David Porter, Tanya Joosten, Justin Reich, Michael Hannafin, David Wiley, Marilena Aspioti, and Nikos Aspiotis

At Royal Roads University, my colleagues have supported me in innumerable ways to complete this work. These colleagues include: Jo Axe, Doug Hamilton, Samantha Wood, Robynne Devine, Deborah Zornes, Mary Bernard, Matt Heinz, and Steve Grundy.

This work would not have been possible without the support of my research assistants and post-doctoral associates. Either by contributing directly to this research or indirectly supporting my research agenda, their help has been invaluable. These are: Rich McCue, Laura Pasquini, Cesar Navarrete, Bonnie Stewart, and Gregory Russell. I am indebted to Bonnie Stewart who edited large sections of this book and helped write two of the narratives that appear in it.

My students, in Canada, the UK, and the US, with their insightful questions, their eagerness to learn, and their inquisitive nature have helped keep me motivated and on my toes – and I appreciate them for that.

Royal Roads University and the University of Texas at Austin supported various activities pertaining to this investigation including funding for dissemination and outreach. The STELLAR Fellowship Mobility Program also provided support for this research. I also am incredibly indebted to the Canada Research Chairs program for the support it provided to my research endeavors.

Writing appearing in this book has appeared elsewhere in different forms, and I am fortunate to have had the permission to edit and republish various parts of that work into this book. Specifically, chapter 2, Networked Scholarship, draws heavily on: Veletsianos, G. & Kimmons, R. (2012b). Networked Participatory Scholarship: Emergent techno-cultural pressures toward open and digital scholarship in online networks. *Computers & Education, 58*(2), 766–774.

The book also draws from the findings, implications/discussion, and conclusion sections of or contains reprinted content from the following papers:

Veletsianos, G. (2012). Higher education scholars' participation and practices on Twitter. *Journal of Computer Assisted Learning, 28*(4), 336–349. John Wiley & Sons, Inc.
Veletsianos, G. (2013). Open practices and identity: Evidence from researchers and educators' social media participation. *British Journal of Educational Technology, 44*(3), 639–651. John Wiley & Sons, Inc.
Veletsianos, G. & Kimmons, R. (2012a). Assumptions and challenges of open scholarship. *The International Review of Research in Open and Distance Learning, 13*(4), 166–189. Athabasca University.
Veletsianos, G. & Kimmons, R. (2012b). Networked Participatory Scholarship: Emergent technocultural pressures toward open and digital scholarship in online networks. *Computers & Education, 58*(2), 766–774. Elsevier.
Veletsianos, G. & Kimmons, R. (2013). Scholars and faculty members' lived experiences in online social networks. *The Internet and Higher Education, 16*(1), 43–50. Elsevier.

1

INTRODUCTION

In this book, I explore the practices and experiences of the educational scholar on social media and online networks. My goal is to help you understand scholars' participation in online spaces and, in doing so, provide a lens through which you can problematize the presence of social media and online networks, or lack thereof, in the life of the contemporary scholar.

Educational scholars are doctoral students, instructors, researchers, and professors. While scholarly practice may traditionally be viewed as scientific discovery, its meaning in this book is broader, and will be explored further in the next few pages. For now, any reference to the term *scholarship* in this book should be understood to include both teaching and research activities (Boyer, 1990; Hutchings & Shulman, 1999).

Commonplace technological activities in scholars' lives include the use of bibliographic management software, data analysis tools, and transcription services. Social media and online networks appear to be less popular with scholars, but academic-focused online social networks Academia.edu, ResearchGate, and Mendeley boast 11, 4.5, and 3.1 million users worldwide respectively (VanNoorden, 2014). Other reports note that scholars often use Twitter, YouTube, Facebook, LinkedIn and personal blogs (Lupton, 2014; Moran, Seaman, Tinti-Kane, 2011).

What scholars might do on these sites varies. A cultural anthropologist, for instance, might share draft versions of her research on her blog, a geographer might post his syllabus on a document-sharing website, and a political scientist might investigate relationships between social media participation and election results. Using such tools as blogs and online social networks may enable scholars to remain current in their research field, explore new approaches to teaching via networking with colleagues, interact with individuals mentioning their research/ work, and expose their work to larger audiences.

Scholars who make use of participatory technologies and online social networks to share, improve, validate, and further their scholarship engage in *networked scholarship* and in this book are described as *networked scholars*. Similar practices are enacted under the labels open scholarship, social scholarship, and digital scholarship, though these descriptors differ from networked scholarship in significant ways.

Although some of the statistics regarding scholar participation on social media are impressive, there are very few reports presenting the stories behind the numbers, describing scholars' experiences and activities, and telling the story of social media in academia. While a high percentage of faculty may be using social media, what are they actually doing with it? Are they using social media to change the ways they engage in scholarship? Or, are social media co-opted and used in familiar ways, and in the process, being stripped of their affordances? What is it like to use social media as a scholar? What do scholars share and how do they represent themselves online? What obstacles and challenges do they face?

The argument that permeates this book is that scholars' experiences and practices on social media and online networks are not well understood and the evidence describing their experiences is limited and fragmented. My thesis is that a lack of understanding of networked scholarship and social media use is detrimental to scholars, institutions, and scholarly practice. I'm not suggesting that you should be on social media or that social media will impact practice in positive ways. Rather, I'm urging you to understand online networks in the context of scholarly practice, so that you can investigate how they are experienced and used. In doing so, I hope that you will consider how social media and online networks may be changing practice *and* how existing practices shape the ways social media are used.

In 1987, Papert argued that users and teachers of LOGO (an educational programming language) need to "be able to talk about LOGO, to criticize it, and to discuss other people's criticisms." They should be able to do more than just use and teach the language. Papert argued that technocentric questions such as "Does the computer (or LOGO or whatever) produce thinking skills?" are foolish.

In the same way, this book rejects technocentric and technodeterministic perspectives pertaining to the use of social media for scholarship. When the question, "What do scholars need to know about networked scholarship?" arises in the future, my hope is that you will be able to look beyond the question of "what social media and online networks can do *for* scholarship." Rather, in aligning with Papert's thoughts, I hope that you will be able to say that scholars need to be able to talk about social media, to criticize them, and to discuss other people's criticisms.

To that end, this book is unique because it differs from other books focusing on social media in education and digital scholarship in two significant ways:

First, this is not a how-to book. You will find no advice in this book about how to create a blog, use Twitter effectively, or, more generally, use social media to share your research, engage students, or increase your citations.

Second, this book does not advocate for networked scholarship. My goal is to understand and problematize the concept of networked scholarship and its implications, not to convince you to enact (or reject) networked scholarship.

The relationship between technology and scholarship has attracted little empirical attention in the education literature even though it has been claimed that "participatory internet technologies ... have the potential to change the way academics engage in scholarship" (Greenhow, Robelia, & Hughes, 2009, p. 252) and that "information technology and the 'consumerization of everything' may represent both the greatest opportunity for scholars and scholarship in human history *and* the greatest threat to the scholarly enterprise in the thousand-year history of the Western university" (Katz, 2010, p. 48). Kumashiro et al., (2005, p. 276) warned the education community about these issues, noting that "technological changes are going to flood how we currently think about, do, and represent research" and noted that the use of technology for scholarship "is being largely ignored in colleges of education, other than in simplistic and trivial ways." This book rectifies the lack of attention the topic has received.

Why Is This Topic Significant?

While social media/networks have been both extolled and decried in the academic literature and the popular press, a greater understanding of the experiences and practices of scholars with social media and online networks is necessary for a number of reasons.

First, social media and online networks appeal to scholars in a never-ending array of disciplines. From psychiatrists to education scholars, from biologists to mathematicians, it seems that the potential (and drawbacks) of social media are debated across disciplinary lines. For instance, the following abstract is published in a journal aimed at cognitive scientists, but little else in this abstract (and subsequent article) is unique to cognitive science:

> Cognitive scientists are increasingly using online social media, such as blogging and Twitter, to gather information and disseminate opinion, while linking to primary articles and data. Because of this, Internet tools are driving a change in the scientific process, where communication is characterised by rapid scientific discussion, wider access to specialist debates, and increased cross-disciplinary interaction. This article serves as an introduction to and overview of this transformation.
>
> *(Stafford & Bell, 2012, p. 489)*

Second, the increasing use of technological solutions for educational and scholarly purposes without an empirical understanding and evaluation of that use engenders several pitfalls and shortcomings. These dangers are particularly relevant in the face of rejuvenated claims regarding the potential of technological and scholarly innovations to transform practice when past empirical evidence suggests that panaceas to educational problems are rarely successful (Cuban, 2001; Tennyson, 1994). This book therefore responds to the call by Selwyn and Grant (2009) to study the actual use of innovations as opposed to their potential. An evidence-based understanding of scholars' digital practices will facilitate the development of educational and scholarly approaches that are sensitive to what it means to learn, teach, and research online and may foster further innovations in how individuals and institutions enact digital and networked practices.

Third, there is an almost universal recognition that higher education is at a critical junction and that educational institutions worldwide are facing enormous challenges. Given that social media and online networks permeate contemporary cultures, they may present promising opportunities for addressing a number of these challenges. An evidence-based understanding of scholars' efforts, experiences, obstacles, and tensions with networked scholarship might help contribute to a greater understanding of the role of digital technology in the enterprise of higher education, especially as open/digital/networked scholarship, frequently performed via social media, is seen as a radical breakthrough in how new knowledge is created and shared (Nielsen, 2012; Weller, 2011).

Fourth, there's something unique about social media – not necessarily about the technology that connects people to one another and to information – but about the ways that social media are "intertwined with neoliberal capitalism and data surveillance" (boyd, 2015) while being pervasive in higher education settings. While social in nature, the commercial nature of these technologies and the affordances they provide to observe and scrutinize others raises conundrums for individual scholars and academia alike.

A Note on the Book's Structure

This book is divided into twelve chapters. Each chapter follows a similar structure, starting with a set of questions or a narrative/story illustrating some of the issues under investigation. Next, the phenomenon is described, and supportive evidence is presented. Each chapter is summarized below.

1. Introduction

This is the chapter you are currently reading, wherein I introduce the book and the significance of networked scholarship.

2. Networked Scholarship

In this chapter, I describe the concept of networked scholarship – the foundation of this book – and describe (a) the relationships between technology and scholarship, and (b) the technocultural pressures that exist to raise the profile of networked scholarship.

3. Anna: A Social Media Advocate

In this chapter, I present an interview with Anna, a scholar who uses social media extensively in her practice.

4. Networks of Knowledge Creation and Dissemination

I describe how scholars are using online networks to engage in knowledge creation and dissemination. I describe how academics use networks to do and share research and present examples of academics doing research online, reaching new understandings, and supporting communities in creating knowledge.

5. Jaime: The Complicated Realities of Day-to-Day Social Media Use

In this chapter, Jaime describes the complicated nature of day-to-day social media use.

6. Networks of Tension and Conflict

In participating online, scholars face tensions, challenges, and conundrums, and I use this chapter to explore and investigate these.

7. Nicholas: A Visitor

In this chapter, I present a description of Nicholas, a composite character I developed to demonstrate how the majority of academics currently use social media and technologies.

8. Networks of Inequity

In this chapter, I argue that some individuals may be more capable of exploiting social media than others as a result of a number of factors (e.g., power, wealth). This argument calls into question whether social media truly are the equalizing forces they are sometimes portrayed to be.

9. Networks of Disclosure

Academics have used social media and online networks to disclose intimate details of their lives (e.g., their struggles with debilitating diseases) and seek out support that they don't find at their institutions. In this chapter, I discuss scholars' disclosures and experiences of care.

10. Fragmented Networks

In this chapter, I explain that scholars' identity online consists of a constellation of identity fragments. I argue that what individuals observe on social media is neither fully representative of authentic identity nor fully performative.

11. Scholarly Networks, or Scholars in Networks?

In this chapter I argue that to understand scholars' online lives, researchers need to examine more than scholarly practices online and need to explore scholars' digital activities and participation in an expansive way.

12. Conclusion

I conclude by discussing broader implications that we can draw from the investigation presented in this book.

2

NETWORKED SCHOLARSHIP

What is networked scholarship? What is its relationship with technology and openness? How does it differ from open, digital, and social scholarship? What are the sociocultural and technological pressures for scholarship to be more "networked?" In this chapter, I explain what I mean by networked participatory scholarship (or, networked scholarship) and describe the relationships between technology and scholarship. But first, a personal story.

THE COUCHES OF STRANGERS

It's 2005. I'm a graduate student at the University of Minnesota and I live in the always beautiful, but often frigid, city of Minneapolis.

Though I don't always enjoy driving, I am particularly fond of road trips and the opportunities they provide for learning about the world. That summer, my girlfriend and I decided to take a road trip from Minnesota to Tennessee following the roads that run parallel to the Mississippi River. The Great River Road they call it – a network of local, state, and federal roads that showcase the beauty of the states bordering the Mississippi River.

A few months prior to this trip I discovered Couchsurfing.com, and this site generated one of my early experiences with modern social media. "Couchsurfing" refers to spending a night or two on the couch of a stranger. The website facilitated interactions between individuals who were interested in hosting others and individuals who were interested in spending nights on someone else's couch.

Given my mild disdain of driving long distances, my girlfriend and I divided our trip in such a way so as to limit daily driving to 4 to 6 hours. We arranged for accommodations driving south toward Tennessee because we wanted to follow the Great River Road, but we decided to return back to Minneapolis via a different route so as to visit more states.

Using Couchsurfing.com, we found two individuals who were willing to host us: one in Diamond City, Arkansas, and one in Kansas City, Kansas.

An elderly couple was willing to let us sleep on their couch in Diamond City, a city we knew nothing about. Once we arrived we learned that Diamond City is a small retirement town – a destination only for those visiting their parents who retire there.

We arrived in Diamond City around 5pm. We stopped at one of the two local diners prior to joining our hosts so as to have an early dinner and pre-empt being a burden to them. Our hosts were welcoming and friendly, and we spent the next few hours in their living room getting to know one another.

During the conversation, we learned that our hosts were as unsure as we were of this arrangement. We were the first people who had reached out to them through the couchsurfing website, and, while they were apprehensive at first, they decided to host us, as we seemed to be "just a couple of kids from the Midwest."

Eventually we made our way to the porch. We continued our conversation, enjoying a beautiful August night, until ten or so of their friends joined us. They brought their chairs and musical instruments and we quickly learned that our hosts' friends were preparing a "hootenanny" for us. A hootenanny – an informal gathering involving folk music and dancing – was as foreign to me as I was to them. We spent many hours dancing, learning about what life is like in a small retirement town, and discussing the demise of small-town America.

Our hosts' generosity and hospitality stayed with me. These individuals were not only willing to make themselves vulnerable and share their house with us for the night, they also went out of their way to organize a fun event and share this aspect of their life with us. The next morning, a group of our hosts' friends prepared breakfast, and we left for our next couchsurfing destination: Kansas City, Kansas.

Dave, our gracious Kansas City host, invited his friends to have dinner and drinks with us, gave us a tour of Kansas City, and offered us his bed instead of the couch: He had painted his living room the night before and the smell of paint was still lingering. "Guests don't need to be exposed to toxic fumes," he argued, and we reluctantly agreed to sleep on his bed while he enjoyed the couch – and the paint smell – for the night.

When I share these two stories with others, I often face puzzling looks and questions regarding my sanity. "What if your host was an axe murderer?" someone asked me once. "And you really don't know these people?" is another question I am asked often. While the idea of sleeping on a stranger's couch may not be appealing to everyone, and may sound a bit too trusting, all my limbs are still intact.

These stories demonstrate the power and potential of networks and openness. Supported by the web as a social platform that allows individuals to consume, produce, remix, and contribute content without the need for specialized technical know-how, networks call into question the assumptions many of us have been conditioned to make about life, work, and others. Social media – the technologies which have come to represent online networks in the twenty-first century – have become part of the fabric of contemporary societies and our educational systems. Worldwide experiences with social media suggest that these technologies facilitate the transformation of various aspects of common culture in both intentional and unexpected ways. For instance, as news agencies adopt social media to engage audiences and increase revenues, they are simultaneously reporting on instances where the use of social networking sites has led to harm. News stories describing how networks of strangers have made a positive difference in people's lives are eclipsed by stories of how criminal networks use technology to organize and stories of teenage cyber bullying.

Social media have also penetrated higher education, and have influenced not only the ways students connect with each other, but also the ways scholarship is organized, delivered, enacted, and experienced (Weller, 2011). In scholars' lives, networks may call into question some of the foundational assumptions scholars operate under, including assumptions about teaching, research, knowledge production/dissemination, and the academy itself.

For example, networked scholarship is often associated with the concept of openness. Openness refers to the proposition that various scholarly resources (e.g., textbooks, syllabi, publications, data) should be governed by licensing policies that provide others with free and perpetual permissions to retain, reuse, revise, remix, and redistribute the work (Wiley, 2015). Openness suggests that data used in research should be published with open licenses so that other researchers can use them; textbooks should be published with open licenses so that instructors can mix and match them to meet their needs; and instructional activities and syllabi should be shared with licenses that allow others to use them, revise them, and share them again – perhaps even benefiting the original sharer as a result of the revision.

Openness is often amplified by digital technology. To illustrate its potential consider the example of a single copy of a physical text placed on reserve in the library. Use of the text is rivalrous: if one student has the copy, other students do not. Digital technology, however, allows multiple copies of the book to be made and shared, and use of one digital copy does not preclude others from using the same copy. In this way distribution may occur more widely and fairly, leading advocates to claim that open practices may "broaden access to education and knowledge, reduce costs, enhance the impact and reach of scholarship and education, and foster the development of more equitable, effective, efficient, and transparent scholarly and educational processes" (Veletsianos & Kimmons, 2012a).

I used Couchsurfing.com once more when I was living in the UK in 2009. I was going to spend a few days in Faro, Portugal, and had sent the following note to my potential host:

> Dear Eric,
>
> I am writing in the hopes that you will be interested in hosting me on your couch for 2 nights. I can see from your profile that it's your birthday on May 2nd, and I would completely understand if you have something else planned.
>
> A little bit about me: I live in the UK and teach at the University of Manchester. I lived in the United States (Minneapolis) for 8 years, but I am originally from Cyprus. I speak Greek and English and love to explore and travel, learn about different cultures, photography, music, beer, and good company. I am very friendly and considerate and am looking forward to visiting Portugal for the first time!
>
> Please look at my profile and if there's anything that you would like to know, please feel free to ask!

Within a few hours, Eric responded and noted that he had birthday plans and I should join. Specifically, he and his friends were having a party on an island off the coast of Faro and I should join them. The party was starting on the 1st and ending on the 3rd and as long as I didn't mind "sleeping on the floor or even on the beach" Eric was happy to host me.

What Does Couchsurfing Have to Do with Networked Scholarship?

The thought of spending a night on a stranger's couch may elicit apprehension and concern from many, just as the thought of spending time online may elicit trepidation from scholars. In the same way that our hosts in Arkansas were apprehensive about opening their home to strangers, scholars may be apprehensive about opening their research to the broader public. Other scholars may worry about the time commitment necessary to engage in activities not traditionally valued by their universities, such as social media outreach. The practice of networked scholarship isn't without perils.

In addition to posing risks, however, both couchsurfing and networked scholarship offer opportunities for growth, as well: couchsurfing may allow people from different cultures to get to know one another; networked scholarship can enable scholars from disparate disciplines to meet and collaborate. Alternatively, both activities may have relatively mundane outcomes: sleeping on a stranger's couch does not necessarily mean that one will have a life-changing experience in the same way that going online does not mean that one will find a large audience eager to consume one's research. "I was disappointed that my research didn't go viral after I joined Twitter" one professor told me.

Effective couchsurfing or networked scholarship may require particular literacies for successful participation. And while advocacy for the benefits of open, social, and digital scholarship features prominently in the literature (Kimmons, 2014), and encouragement to engage with emergent forms of scholarship is pervasive, the reality on the ground is different: scholars' activities on social media are both exceptional and mundane, and their experiences may be both inspiring and harrowing. Above all, however, such experiences are neither universal nor pre-determined.

As social media and openness become increasingly popular, sharing economies gain hold, and online networks permeate every aspect of life, social, cultural, and technological tensions affect the scholarly enterprise and the work that educators and researchers do. This relationship between academic practices and technologies is negotiated and complex. It can be framed via three perspectives.

The first perspective suggests that social media (and their design and affordances) shape scholarship and participation. This is the technological deterministic perspective that is often revealed in narratives pertaining to social media having an impact on scholarship. Institutional encouragement to use social media with the implication that such use will increase scholarly reach and citations falls under this perspective.

The second viewpoint suggests that teaching and scholarship (and the structures, rewards, and overall practices permeating academia) shape how social media are used. This perspective reflects a social shaping of technology approach. This perspective recognizes that networked scholarly practices are shaped by social, cultural, economic, and political factors, rejecting the notion that technologies (and practices) are deterministic. Use of technology to support traditional practices (e.g., using a blog as a website in which to deposit peer-reviewed publications) reflects this viewpoint.

The third perspective is an extension of the second and anticipates that academics adapt and appropriate social media to fulfill personal and professional desires and values. This perspective holds that, with adequate information and evidence, learners, instructors, and researchers have the agency to accept or reject any particular technology or to find alternative uses for it that will better serve their needs. Such agency is recognized in scholars' strategic uses of technology in scholarship broadly, and in teaching and research in particular.

These three perspectives are often unstated, but permeate the literature and conversations pertaining to social media use in education and scholarship.

Changing Notions of Scholarship

In recent years, scholars in many disciplines have recognized the necessity to expand definitions of scholarship to encompass aspects of the profession that extend beyond strict notions of scientific discovery. For example,

- Pellino, Blackburn, and Boberg (1984) proposed an expanded definition of scholarship that includes (a) professional activity, (b) research/publication, (c) artistic endeavors, (d) engagement with novel ideas, (e) community service, and (f) pedagogy.
- Unsworth (2000) suggested that scholars engage in "scholarly primitives" that are common across disciplines, and these are the practices of discovering, annotating, comparing, referring, sampling, illustrating, and representing.
- Palmer, Teffeau, and Pirmann (2009) suggested that scholars engage in the activities of searching, collecting, reading, writing, and collaborating.

Beyond these specific activities, Boyer (1990) summarized scholarly practice in terms of the scholarship of discovery, the scholarship of integration, the scholarship of application, and the scholarship of teaching. Boyer's view of scholarship was proposed as a result of his empirical evaluation of scholars' activities in higher education which led him to argue that this perspective better describes the types of activities that scholars engage with because knowledge is generated and acquired not just through research, but through teaching as well. In fact, Boyer's framework of scholarship is often used as a starting point for defining scholarly practices in the digital age and a number of authors have sought to update Boyer's model to reflect contemporary thinking relating to scholarly practice (e.g., Garnet & Ecclesfield, 2011; Greenhow & Gleason, 2014; Heap & Minocha, 2012; Pearce et al., 2010; Stewart, 2015a; Weller, 2011).

The movement to develop expanded definitions of scholarship comes in response to a widespread over-reliance upon strict notions of scientific research within universities to define scholarly practice. As Popovich and Abel (2002) explain, this may stem from the identifying of scholars in terms of specific disciplines rather than the goals of the academy at large. Boshier (2009) further argues that the current state of scholarly culture and practice is being largely framed by a narrow neoliberalism in which deep, contemplative research has been rejected in favor of "just-in-time" scholarship and a questionable faith in various persistent structures of the academy. Latour (2004) expresses similar concerns by noting that certain aspects of scholarly work have moved beyond internal criticism.

Although scholars in many fields have sought for an expansion of scholarship, traction is rife with difficulties emerging from many areas, not least the "orthodoxies of higher education" (Boshier, p. 2).

The Shared History of Scholarship and Technology

While contemporary conversations pertaining to emergent forms of scholarship frequently highlight the suggestion that contemporary technologies provide many opportunities to rethink scholarly practice, it's important to pause and ask: how have pre-digital technological innovations influenced both the scholarly work of professional researchers and the universities which housed them?

The history of scholarship is largely intertwined with the history of technological innovation, as well as social and religious development. By considering how technology has influenced the development of scholarship into its current state, we may gain insights into how further developments in technology might further propel scholarship into new directions. Consider these words of Binkley (1935, ¶ 1) over seventy years ago: "There is [currently] taking place … a series of changes more revolutionary in their possible impact upon culture than the invention of printing." At the time, Binkley noted how mass publishing (a technological innovation that had diffused prior to his writing) had largely changed the culture of scholarly work. He argued that several centuries before, with the invention of the printing press, scholarly materials that had largely been inaccessible to those interested in doing scholarly work were made readily available to both professional and amateur scholars alike. Whereas the canon of scholarly resources had previously only been held in monasteries and libraries, the printing press made duplication of those materials so easy that they soon became accessible to a far larger group of scholars than was previously possible. Binkley explains that through the technological innovation of printing "it became possible for the moderately wealthy man to possess what previously only princes or great religious establishments could afford – a fairly complete collection of the materials he desired," which brought about a cultural shift in the realm of scholarship by opening it up to a far greater number of scholars (¶ 7).

Greater access, however, was reversed in the early nineteenth century "by the flood of books and journals that accompanied specialization in all fields of learning" and by the mass publishing of scholarly work (¶ 8). Whereas in the past the "moderately wealthy" could keep pace with "princes" and "religious establishments" by purchasing common scholarly works, due to the exponential growth in scholarly works, the only scholars who could keep pace with the mass publishing of specialized field data were those who had direct access to a university with resources sufficient to continually purchase recurring publications that were extremely diverse and specialized. Thus, Binkley explains that "the qualities of the printing process that began in the fifteenth century to make things accessible have now begun in our different circumstances to make them inaccessible," leading to the death of the "amateur scholar" and the shift of research from the realm of an "honored sport" to that of an "exclusive profession" (¶ 9).

Ultimately, though Binkley's heralding of "revolutionary" technological innovations such as microphotography and "near-print" replication may not have panned out as he had anticipated, what we can learn from Binkley is that the culture of scholarship has historically been refined, or even changed, by technological innovation. Additionally, certain, though not all, technological innovations have the capacity to lead to a fundamental rethinking of how scholarship is done, but this rethinking may not occur in anticipated ways. Upon revisiting Binkley's work twelve years later, Tate (1947) points out that though microphotography did not lead to the rebirth of the amateur scholar, as Binkley had hoped and anticipated, it did create new issues in scholarship that would fundamentally change how research was done. Given the "oceans of documentation" which emerged from some of Binkley's technologies, researchers found themselves "confronted" and "confounded" by the amount of data now available to them, which led to a rethinking of the role of scholarly aides as guided assistants who waded through the vast number of available reports and articles.

This explosion of data also led to a simultaneous rethinking of the role of the professor as a mentor and manager of supporting aides rather than as a lone scholar, and the effects of such technological innovations have continued to be seen in how scholarly research has developed up to the current time. In the words of Siemens and Matheos (2010, ¶ 9), "universities have always intersected with the society in which they are domiciled and have, to a certain extent, changed with society, culminating in the contemporary ... university." The development of the contemporary university reflects a rich history of interaction between the institution, society, and available technology tools, lending credence to the notion that just as societies, governments, and other social groups adapt and change over time, so too do universities, the work that they do, and how they do that work. In short, the development of the university is intertwined with the development of other aspects of society (Alexander, 2007; Rhoads & Liu, 2009; Siemens & Matheos, 2010).

Technology as an Artifact of Culture

As digital technologies are becoming increasingly prevalent, we have begun to witness similar transformations in the ways that scholars use networking technologies to share and collaborate; publishers use online spaces to collect, review, and disseminate research articles; and educators use social media and networking technologies to enhance various aspects of their teaching. As technologies change and cultures shift, so too do the literacies and skills necessary to operate in professional contexts. For instance, Jenkins et al. (2009) suggest that due to the proliferation of emerging technologies and their effects on the world, in order to successfully participate in the world, individuals need to develop a new set of competencies that include skills such as appropriation, transmedia navigation, and networking. As scholars similarly find themselves confronted with the challenges of emerging technologies and shifting cultures, they too are being led to adapt and acquire new competencies in order to function in their changing world.

We should be careful, however, in attributing causation to technology with regard to shifts in scholarly culture. Technology may just as validly be seen as a reflection of cultural trends as a cause of them. In the case of the printing press discussed above, for instance, it may just as equally be stated that the printing press came about as a result of a widespread cultural belief in the value of accessibility as the reverse. Thus, inferring causality between technology and culture remains a fuzzy issue. As a more modern example, Solum (2006) argues that the growing practice of legal blogging is an effect – a symptom of how legal scholarship has already changed – and not a cause of cultural changes. Similarly, rather than asking how emerging technologies will transform the culture of education scholarship, we could ask what the emergence and use of such tools as Facebook, Twitter, mobile devices, and so forth reveals about scholars in both a cultural sense (with regard to how knowledge in our culture has come to be acquired, tested, validated, and shared) as well as within the subculture of the university.

A similar argument has been made about other innovations. Most significantly for our purposes, Peter and Deimann (2013) argued that openness is as much a social, economic, and cultural phenomenon as it is a technological one. As an example to illustrate this premise, they argue that books, sevententh-century coffeehouses, and mail services – developments that supported the opening of education – were developed partly because society deemed them to be important, and not simply because technological innovations made them possible.

I approach the rest of the book on the premise that technology and culture influence and reflect one another in complicated, and often unexpected, ways. By doing so, I hope to problematize conventional thinking around the role and impact of technology on scholarship, and highlight how scholars' lives intersect with networked technologies.

Networked Participatory Scholarship (or, Networked Scholarship)

Networked participatory scholarship (NPS) or *networked scholarship* is the emergent practice of scholars' use of social technologies and online social networks to pursue, share, reflect upon, critique, improve, validate, and further their scholarship (Veletsianos & Kimmons, 2012b). The ways that scholars use digital technologies to support scholarship includes a set of practices and dispositions that have the potential to fundamentally alter the way we view scholarship. This practice is becoming increasingly visible even though by all accounts it is at an early stage of adoption and development within the scholarly community. As a very basic example,

academic-oriented social networking sites provide scholars with the opportunity to retrieve data pertaining to their participation and in relation to documents they post online, gaining a more nuanced picture of the reach of their scholarship than what they could accomplish in a pre-digital era. Figure 2.1 for instance, shows web analytics from a social networking site for academics. This page shows how many times this scholar's profile and uploaded documents were viewed in the last thirty days; shows how many unique individuals visited the scholar's profile in the last 30 days; and breaks down these numbers on a daily basis. Such data are available to account-holders without the need for a technical know-how.

Over the past few years, there has been growing interest in emergent forms of technology-supported scholarship as some scholars have sought to make their research accessible faster and cheaper. A number of researchers have noted the value of technology in fostering scholarship that is characterized as digital, social, and open (Burton, 2009; Cohen, 2007; Greenhow, 2009; Oblinger, 2010; Pearce et al., 2010; Weller 2009). Borgman (2007) describes *digital scholarship* as using technology to enhance scholarly practice and collaboration. Cohen (2007, ¶ 1) notes that *social scholarship* "is the practice … in which the use of social tools is an integral part of the research and publishing process [and is characterized by] openness, conversation, collaboration, access, sharing, and transparent revision." *Open scholarship* on the other hand focuses on the wide and broad dissemination of scholarship by a variety of interconnected means (e.g., technology, licensing) aiming to broaden knowledge and reduce barriers to access to knowledge and information (Veletsianos & Kimmons, 2012a).

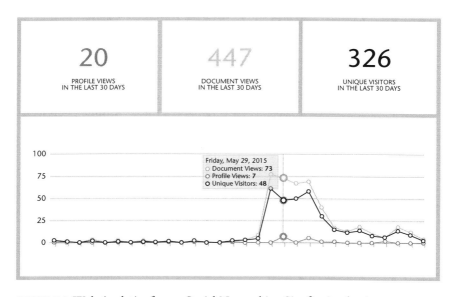

FIGURE 2.1 Web Analytics from a Social Networking Site for Academics

The scholars that enact these practices are often described as "social scholars" or "open scholars," but even though individual authors' definitions may vary slightly from one another depending upon the scholarly behaviours they are emphasizing, such definitions tend to focus on a few common components, including technology, collaboration, sharing, and openness (Burton, 2009; Cohen, 2007; Weller, 2009). For example, Cohen presents a list of fourteen characteristics that describe social scholars (e.g., "a social scholar initiates or joins an online community devoted to her topic, using any of a number of social software services or tools," ¶ 4). Burton argues that "the Open Scholar is someone who makes their intellectual projects and processes digitally visible and who invites and encourages ongoing criticism of their work and secondary uses of any or all parts of it – at any stage of its development" (¶ 5). The visions presented for these kinds of scholars contrast to the dominant conceptualization of scholarly practices which are often seen as monastic and lacking ongoing participation, support, and conversation (Kumashiro et al., 2005). While it could be argued that scholars have always shared their work with colleagues (e.g., face-to-face, via correspondence, over the telephone, through conferences), and disciplines have always had open (and less open) scholars, some of the questions that we need to consider are the following:

- How are the (ongoing and new) needs and values of scholars supported by new technologies and participatory practices?
- As societies change in significant ways, how is scholarship changing in response?
- How do current conceptualizations of scholarly practice and online participation hinder scholarly goals?
- How do online networks, and the ability to have instant and continuous access to networks of colleagues, impact the ways that scholars research and teach?
- How may the larger and diverse audiences found on public online social networks impact and interact with the work that scholars do?

While early adopters often extol the benefits of new technologies, attempts at using technology to enhance scholarly practice have so far been met with skepticism and reluctance. As departmental requirements for tenure and promotion in institutions of higher education remain unchanged (Ayers, 2004; Kiernan, 2000; Purdy & Walker, 2010), for many faculty members the potential value of "going digital" has not been worth risking tenure and departmental stigma (Ayers, ¶ 18). Though scholars and their universities may generally look upon digital scholarship with a receptive air (Kiernan, 2000), Andersen (2003) shows that departmental acceptance has been found to vary by discipline, with the hard sciences being the most receptive, followed by the social sciences and the humanities. The reason for such differing levels of acceptance may largely be due to what is being done by scholars in the current formulation of digital scholarship. As Borgman (2007) points out, much of the effect that digitization has had upon scholarship revolves around the blurring of primary and secondary sources, wherein primary sources (i.e., data sets) are made more widely available to researchers in the form of publications and are more widely being listed on curriculum vitae. In the hard sciences, it is generally suggested that making data sets more widely available would have great value. For instance, providing access to genome mapping data may offer large societal benefits because multiple research teams can analyze such data concurrently. Within the social sciences, however, such motivations for collaboration may be of less interest (cf. Thagard, 1997). Additionally, the publication and dissemination of secondary sources via digitization is much more problematic, as academia lacks an established framework of evaluation for judging the legitimacy or quality of interpretive or positional work that is distributed via non-traditional channels, such as videos on file-sharing sites or multimedia narratives (cf. Borgman, 2007; Purdy & Walker, 2010). Such a framework would need to consider complex aspects of digital publication such as originality, transferability, impact, peer judgements, and usefulness to the field and to society (Andersen, 2003; Kiernan, 2000). As a result, digital scholarship often lacks appeal for scholars in the social sciences.

When considered through another lens, both the value *and* limitation of digital scholarship may lie in its framing of technology through a lens of amplification. Thus, fields that require mass data collection and access have much to gain from the approach, while fields which rely more upon positionality and interpretation of theory (in addition to data) may find that digital tools which focus on improving data sharing do not help them drastically improve existing practice. However, if we consider that technology may replicate, amplify, or transform scholarly practice depending on how it is used (cf. Hughes et al., 2006; King, 2002) then we begin to see that technology may have untapped potential in that it may not just improve what it is scholars are already doing, but rather it may actually *transform* scholarly practice in positive ways. The development of the field of learning analytics illustrates the value of digital scholarship for education and may encourage scholars in the social sciences to engage in practices that the hard sciences have found beneficial, thus fostering adoption of digital scholarship. As technologies and processes are being developed to collect and analyze massive amounts of data, social science scholars may find value in digital tools which focus on improving data sharing and may help them both improve and reimagine existing practice. Further, the field of learning analytics, which Gašević, Dawson, and Siemens (2015, p. 64) describe as a "bricolage field drawing on research, methods, and techniques from numerous disciplines such as learning sciences, data mining, information visualization, and psychology" may encourage the use of practices that academic "immigrants" can bring to a field other than their own (Nissani, 1997). Thus various digital scholarship practices, such as making data sets widely available so that they can be analyzed by others, may encourage education scholars to collaborate with data mining scholars. One example of such activity in digital learning research involves the sharing of primary data on open courses offered by MIT and Harvard (Ho et al., 2014).

If we are to understand how networked scholarship is materializing today, we need to recognize that current trends in the dominant technophilic consumer culture and discussions within scholarly subcultures point to a deep-rooted rethinking of some fundamental beliefs upon which scholarly structures are built. I examine these trends in the sections that follow and discuss how these emergent factors exert pressures for the adoption of networked scholarship and the rethinking of scholarly practice.

Pressures in the Dominant Culture for Scholarship to Change

Much has changed in the world since the widespread introduction of the Internet and later the social and participatory web. These changes have affected how we make and spend money, how we communicate, how we work, how we collaborate, how we play, how we create and sustain relationships, how we talk (e.g., we take "selfies" and "google" things), and how we find and validate information. What are the implications for scholarly practice when everyone is able to contribute information using tools such as Twitter, YouTube, and Facebook and when technologies that we use on a daily basis, such as our cell phones, capture and archive staggering amounts of data?

Within scholarly circles, the effects of these changes have been experienced in varying degrees. One of the most important of these changes, insofar as networked scholarship is concerned, relates to an emergent emphasis upon collaborative work in the form of "collectives" or aggregations of the actions of individuals that are organized in a complex manner to benefit those individuals (Dron & Anderson, 2009). As Bull et al. (2008, p. 100) explain, online "[c]ollaborative projects such as Wikipedia demonstrate that a previously unexploited collective intelligence can be tapped when the right conditions are established," and the resultant collective artifacts of these exploits have the potential of spurring innovation.

As a culture, we have quickly found great value in online collaborative projects. The English-language Wikipedia alone, for instance, boasts a collection of 4.8 million articles collectively written by distributed individuals (Wikipedia, 2015), and it has consistently remained in the list of the top ten most visited sites on the Internet (Alexa Top 500 Global Sites, 2015). Firefox, as another example, is a community-developed web browser that has been the most popular or second most popular web browsing software in the world since 2005 (Browser Statistics, 2015). Further, even though lay users may not explicitly recognize other collective software products which they use on a daily basis, by virtue of the fact that the average Internet user employs web server technologies to open web pages and to access content, we, as an Internet-using community, have found great implicit value in other open and collaborative projects like Apache, GNU/Linux, PHP, MySQL, and Python which are widespread in web server environments. Though such collective projects may have been initiated by a relatively small number of technological savants, collectivist models of development and production have diffused into a multiplicity of realms. "Wiki," for instance, has quickly become a common word as several platforms have emerged and been adopted as valuable information-sharing platforms (e.g. Mediawiki, FederatedWiki, etc). A further outgrowth of this phenomenon can be seen more generally in the emerging interest in many fields to study the development and growth of online networks and communities, by which we seek to understand the reality and implications of our interdependence (Briggle & Mitcham, 2009).

Though causal relationships between technological innovation and culture may be unclear, there seems to be a case for arguing that technological innovation and the way technologies are used in the larger culture influences various subcultures such as academic publishers and research communities. For instance, as academic publishers recognize the role of social media in scholarly practice and the use of generic search engines like Google to discover scholarship, many have published guides for authors to use social media to publicize their work and make it "SEO-friendly," meaning optimized to be found, indexed, and retrieved by search engines (e.g., Elsevier, 2012; SAGE, 2015).

To illustrate using a historical example, though the emergence of the printing press may not have reflected the value systems of *all* scholarly subcultures (e.g., some may have been interested in keeping knowledge sources restricted to elite groups), it could be said that its emergence did reflect the dominant culture of the time (i.e., the common people who were interested in gaining access to knowledge sources), which then influenced elite subcultures. Likewise, it could be argued that though the emergence of technology-driven activities like blogging, social bookmarking, and social networking may not reflect the culture of university scholarship, they may very well reflect aspects of the dominant culture, which then gains power, via the tool, to influence scholarly cultures. Thus, though the relationship between the dominant culture, technology, and subcultures may be ill-understood and extraordinarily complex, it is important to recognize that there is an interplay between the three by which changes in the dominant culture or technology may either reflect or influence transformation in the subculture in a complex and negotiated manner. We should emphasize however, that scholarly work does not exist in a vacuum and that how we view scholarship as a society changes in conjunction with a variety of other factors (e.g., technological innovations, dominant cultural narratives), which are currently and continually in a state of flux.

Pressures among Scholars for Scholarship to Change

Our understanding of scholarship has been in a state of transformation in recent years. For example, education researchers have been asking foundational questions about the nature of their scholarship as they have reflected on the pursuits of educational scholars and what it means to be a scholar in general. Such evaluations of current scholarly practice may be the result of a fundamental re-conceptualization of scholarship that seeks to move away from emphases on disembodied, autonomous practice to community-conscious approaches (Briggle & Mitcham, 2009; Buckley & Du Toit, 2010).

Within the realm of learning theory, a preparatory shift for this realization has gradually come as objectivist epistemologies and behaviorist learning theories have made way for constructivist and socio-constructivist views which hold that knowledge is constructed in the mind of the learner and, as such, cannot exist independently of knowers. This transformed view of the mind from a disembodied and objectivist reasoning tool to an embodied, experiential, and social faculty calls into question the validity of monastic scholarly practices which attempt to disassociate the mind, knowledge, and research from social experience. This view paves the way for rethinking how scholarly knowledge is acquired, expanded, and validated given the embodied, social nature of human experience.

Further, emergent learning approaches which seek to account for increasingly important aspects of social experience in a connected, digital world are coming to the forefront of learning theory discussions. According to connectivist views, for instance, learning is a negotiated, interconnected, cross-disciplinary, and inherently social process within complex environments (Siemens, 2005, 2006). Though many of these ideas regarding learning are not new (Kop & Hill, 2008), and have been discussed by Vygotsky (1978), Lave and Wenger (1991), and others, they are nonetheless attracting growing interest among practitioners and researchers in various forms of learning environments that involve peer instruction and social learning. Such approaches are noteworthy for the mere reason that they break away from norms of twentieth-century university scholarship with regard to fundamental epistemological questions regarding what knowledge is, how it is gained, how it is verified, how it is shared, and how it should be valued. These epistemological reframings of learning take form in scholarly practice in a variety of ways, but they are perhaps most noticeable in how scholars are increasingly beginning to question many heretofore non-negotiable artifacts of the twentieth-century scholarly world.

Peer review is a prime example of how a seemingly non-negotiable scholarly artifact is currently being questioned. While peer review has been a key tool for evaluating scholarly contributions, empirical evidence questions the value and centrality of peer review (Cole, Cole, & Simon, 1981; Rothwell & Martyn, 2000). On the one hand, Neylon and Wu (2009, p. 1) eloquently point out that "the intentions of traditional peer review are certainly noble: to ensure methodological integrity and to comment on potential significance of experimental studies through examination by a panel of objective, expert colleagues" and Scardamalia and Bereiter (2008, p. 9) recognize that "like democracy [peer-review] is recognized to have many faults but is judged to be better than the alternatives." Yet, peer review's harsher critics consider it an anathema. Casadevall and Fang (2009) for instance, question whether peer review is in fact a subtle cousin of censorship that relies heavily upon linguistic negotiation or grammatical "courtship rituals" to determine value, instead of scientific validity or value to the field. Boshier (2009) argues that the current, widespread acceptance of peer review as a valid litmus test for scholarly value is a "faith-" rather than "science-based" approach to scholarship, citing studies in which peer review was found to fail in identifying shoddy work and to succeed in censoring originality. The increased number of research paper retractions that have been recently observed (Fang, Steen, & Casadevall, 2012) also calls into question the value of peer review.

The challenge for scholarly practice is to devise review frameworks that are not just better than the status quo, but that also take into consideration the cultural norms of scholarly activity. Those that fail on the latter front may be doomed from their inception. Reeves (personal communication, May 20, 2015) for example, suggests that double-blind peer-review is ineffective because it is relatively easy for reviewers to decipher an author's identity. He suggests that a more effective and appropriate approach might be for papers to be published immediately and for every living person cited in the manuscript to receive an email inviting him/her to review the published manuscript. An experiment with public peer review online at *Nature,* however, revealed that scholars exhibited minimal interest in online commenting and informal discussions with findings suggesting that scholars "are too busy, and lack sufficient career incentive, to venture onto a venue such as *Nature*'s website and post public, critical assessments of their peers' work" (Nature, 2006, ¶ 9). *Shakespeare Quarterly*, a peer-reviewed scholarly journal founded in 1950, conducted a similar experiment in 2010 (Rowe, 2010). While the trial elicited more interest than the one in *Nature* – more than 40 individuals contributed and, along with the authors, posted more than 300 comments – the experiment further illuminated the fact that tenure considerations impact scholarly contributions. Cohen (2010) reported that "the first question that Alan Galey, a junior faculty member at the University of Toronto, asked when deciding to participate in *Shakespeare Quarterly*'s experiment was whether his essay would ultimately count toward tenure." Notwithstanding the *opportunities* that participatory technologies present for scholarly dialogue, Neylon and Wu (2009) also indicate that papers published in science-related journals with online commenting platforms exhibit a low volume of comments. The issues, these authors suggest, are partly social as scholars (a) lack incentives to spend the time to post comments on online publications and (b) may be unsure of what is appropriate to post in these emergent fora.

Considering the reevaluation of such an entrenched and central structure of scholarly practice as peer review however, we find that the internal values of the scholarly community are shifting in a direction that may be completely incompatible with some of the seemingly non-negotiable elements of twentieth-century scholarship.

Individual scholars' networked activities further illustrate this point: in recent years numerous scholars have engaged in using technological tools in their research, classrooms, and personal lives in ways that differ from twentieth-century paradigms of scholarship (Katz, 2010; Kirkup, 2010). Early adopters continue to use these tools despite incompatibilities with social or institutional structures, because they seem to recognize how such tools have the power to support, amplify, or transform their scholarship in positive ways. Consider how scholars use blogs to support scholarly endeavors. Prior research has identified that blogs are used (a) as debate platforms for scholars who seek to live as public intellectuals, (b) for recording and sharing logs of "pure" research, and (c) as a sort of tongue-in-cheek (often pseudonymous) water cooler around which critical discussions of the scholarly experience can occur (Kirkup, 2010; Walker, 2006). In each of these cases, we see an ideological shift occurring among scholars from established frameworks of academic scholarship and discourse toward structures that are more participatory and empowering, as participation in social media allows the scholar to connect with others (e.g., other scholars, practitioners, the general public) in ongoing discussion and reflection.

Given these growing phenomena, one may wonder: why might scholars be interested in engaging such audiences? Through ethnographic interviews, Nardi, Schiano, and Gumbrecht (2004) found that bloggers use their blogs to "(1) update others on activities and whereabouts, (2) express opinions to influence others, (3) seek others' opinions and feedback, (4) 'think by writing,' and (5) release emotional tension." If this pattern holds true for scholars, then it seems safe to say that a growing number of scholars, as evidenced by an ever-growing number of scholarly blogs, are interested in connecting their scholarship with their identities. Such a connection may serve to frame their research in a way that is increasingly embodied, experiential, and social, as scholars and faculty members use participatory technologies to circumvent established systems that are neither designed to value nor equipped to support such approaches to reflection and inquiry. Couple this with Solum's argument (2006) that the emergence of blogging is a symptom of changing trends in societal thought and values, and it follows that though blogging may not be transforming scholarship per se, growth in academic blogging/tweeting and social digital participation in general may reflect a changing set of values among many scholars regarding their profession. Stewart's (2015b) study of networked scholars found that when scholars go online, their concepts of what counts as scholarship expand to include new, non-institutional terms. In particular, Stewart's participants "articulated concepts of network influence that departed significantly from the codified terms of peer review publication and academic hiring hierarchies on which conventional academic influence is judged" (p. 18). Thus, though participatory technologies may not necessarily serve as catalysts for changing scholarly norms, their growing use by scholars expresses that the current norms of scholarship may be inadequate and may be in a state of change.

Pressures within Scholarly Journals

Even with such changing definitions of scholarship, a discussion on scholarly practice inevitably turns to outlets of scholarly work: the valued media by which scholars connect with the culture that values their work. Technological innovation and cultural shifts have had, and continue to have, an impact on scholarly journals, and developments in this domain parallel the networked scholarly practices described above. These developments can be summarized in three related themes. First, the scholarly world has seen a transition from print-only journals to print and online journals. Second, Open Access publishing has experienced increasing interest. Third, researchers and institutions have sought new ways to evaluate the impact and reach of scholarly work. These issues are examined in detail next.

The dawn of the digital age has had a marked influence on print publishing as stakeholders have realized the benefits afforded by digital dissemination. For example, scholars can access scholarly work published in electronic outlets, such as digital databases, more efficiently, and publishers can make scholarly work available faster than if the work was published in print-only form. In interviewing authors who disseminated their books online for free, Hilton and Wiley (2010) also found that authors perceived that this act enabled them to reach a greater and wider audience, without negatively impacting the sales of their books. Additionally, digital publishing enables alternative forms of content in scholarly work including dynamic content, visualizations, and multimedia integration, such as audio or video interviews (Pearce et al., 2010). The transition to online journals, however, has had further influences on access and journal usage; reports indicate that print journal usage has decreased significantly after the introduction of online journals (De Groote & Dorsch, 2001; Rogers, 2001).

Since the development of the printing press and through the transition to online journals, scholars have embraced methods of broad dissemination of their work. Cultural shifts, such as the Open Access (OA) movement, have shown promise for democratizing access to knowledge and exerted significant pressures on academic publishing. The Budapest Open Access Initiative (2002, ¶ 3) defines OA as literature which is made available for free online,

> permitting any users to read, download, copy, distribute, print, search, or link to the full texts of these articles, crawl them for indexing, pass them as data to software, or use them for any other lawful purpose, without financial, legal, or technical barriers other than those inseparable from gaining access to the Internet itself.

Since the launch of the Educational Resources Information Center (ERIC) in the United States in 1969 as a medium for providing access to education research and information, OA has continued to evolve and has received increased interest in recent years, evidenced in part by the recent wave of higher education institutions passing open access resolutions and mandates requesting faculty to share their scholarly work in an open access manner (Harnad, 2008). For instance, a study of a random sample of 1837 peer-reviewed publications found that 20.4 per cent of them were available for free online either through the publisher's website or through a web search (Björk et al., 2010). While cultural and technological shifts are difficult to differentiate as a result of the fact that they influence each other, in the case of OA, it would have been physically impossible for scholars to make their work available in an OA manner during the age of print publishing. Digital publication provides scholars with the ability to disseminate work without physical or economic barriers.

Peer-reviewed OA journals in the field of education, and the social sciences more broadly, are quickly becoming viable options for scholars to consider (Furlough, 2010; Perkins & Lowenthal, 2015). Scholars have proposed that numerous benefits can be derived from publishing their work in ways that align with the spirit of Open Access. Empirical investigations comparing OA and non-OA academic journals indicate that (a) OA publications tend to be cited more heavily than non-OA (NOA) publications and (b) there is no evidence to suggest that OA publishing harms citations. For instance, Hajjem, Harnad, and Gingras (2005) evaluated 1.3 million articles published in ten disciplines between 1992 and 2003 and found that NOA papers that were self-archived have had more citations than papers that were not self-archived. Eysenbach (2006) reached a similar conclusion in a longitudinal analysis of paper citations, when he found that OA papers were more likely to be cited than NOA papers. Zawacki-Richter, Anderson, and Tuncay (2010) compared six OA and six NOA journals in the field of Distance Education and found no significant differences in terms of citation counts between the two. Additionally, empirical evidence relating to citation metrics indicates that OA articles may be cited earlier than NOA articles (Eysenbach, 2006; Zawacki-Richter, Anderson, & Tuncay, 2010), suggesting that OA may allow faster access to scholarly work and thereby accelerate scholarly dissemination and development.

Finally, researchers and institutions are seeking new ways to evaluate the impact and reach of scholarly work. While scholarly publishing has traditionally been evaluated in terms of impact factors and citation counts (Goodyear et al., 2009), varied technology-informed metrics have recently been proposed in an attempt to more fully capture the influence of scholarly work. For instance, the Public Library of Science (2010) has begun publishing a variety of metrics for each of their publications including article usage statistics (e.g., pageviews), comments/notes/ratings left by article readers, and blog posts citing published articles. Priem and Hemminger (2010) call attention to Scientometrics 2.0 as the idea of using social media to examine journal article use and citations in the participatory nature of the Web. Such data may help scholars gain a more nuanced understanding of the impact and reach of their scholarship, provide transparency to the research community, and allow richer depictions of a scholar's influence.

Conclusion

Higher education institutions face enormous challenges, including a curtailment of public funding, a rise in health care costs for workers and pensioners, an increase in the number of non-traditional students, increasing calls for accountability, and the rise of emerging technologies expected to disrupt the status quo (Christensen, Horn, & Johnson, 2008; Ehrenberg, 2000; Morrison, 2003; Schwier, 2012; Siemens & Matheos, 2010; Thelin, 2013). At the same time, higher education scholars are also confronted by a number of challenges including increased demands to demonstrate the impact of their scholarship (Blyth et al., 2010) and to publish in high quality journals (West & Rich, 2012), while facing an increasingly competitive and uncertain labor market (Åkerlind, 2005; Bauder, 2006; Charfauros & Tierney, 1999; Coalition on the Academic Workforce, 2012).

Scholars are finding themselves in an interesting, but tumultuous, period. A number of high-profile news items in 2013 to 2015 illustrate the tensions, diverse opinions, and strong emotions attached to professors' online participation around networked scholarship. "If you're a professor in Kansas, better stay off the Internet," proclaims the headline on a December 2013 magazine article, following the Kansas Board of Regents decision to adopt guidelines regarding "improper use of social media" that followed a professor's Twitter updates.

But even in the cases where news articles present stories regarding scholars' social media participation, these fall short of the intricate and day-to-day realities that exist in networked practice. And even though recent technological advances provide the foundations and impetus for scholars to productively participate in online scholarly communities and networked scholarship appears to address some of the deficiencies of the status quo, it is imperative to clarify that networked scholarship is neither a panacea, nor a solution without its own shortcomings: networked scholarship challenges academic norms and scholars' participation in networked spaces introduces complexities. Technical skills, such as buying a domain name, creating a blog, or using an RSS aggregator may be the least of a scholar's concerns. Scholarly participation in networked spaces also requires paradigmatic shifts in and evaluation of our identity as scholars, the purposes of education and scholarship, and the academic preparation of scholars.

3

ANNA: A SOCIAL MEDIA ADVOCATE AND NETWORKED SCHOLAR

Having described some of the ways and reasons that scholars use social media, it behooves us to explore in-depth how some scholars might think about social media and networked scholarship. Thus, what follows is an edited interview conducted with a scholar named Anna, a professor of Educational Technology in the United Kingdom. This interview aims to offer readers an insider perspective on how social media have come to be perceived as a meaningful part of one scholar's life.

Anna may not represent the average academic using social media. Her case, though, may be seen as the typical case of a social media user and advocate. Anna is an academic who has embraced and found value in social media and uses it frequently and extensively for professional and personal reasons. She works in a discipline that focuses on technology and as such, she is often surrounded with people who also use social media and are willing to experiment with new tools. While Anna states that social media permeates her life, the intensity of social media use may vary across social media advocates and networked scholars.

In the paragraphs that follow, Anna describes how she uses social media and shares some of her experiences with networked scholarship. It is important to notice that even though Anna has an affinity for social media, she recognizes that tensions might develop in this area. As she describes, she has also experienced some of these tensions. Of special significance are the ways that professional and personal uses of social media intersect.

Interviewer: Could you please describe to me an ordinary day at work as an academic who uses social media? How do you participate on social media, which platforms do you use, and what do you share or communicate?

Anna: This will sound like a grandiose statement, but I think social media has absolutely transformed the way I work as a teacher and as a researcher – absolutely transformed it. When I went to work at Anonymous University in 2006, I'd always seen myself as a bit of an innovator at technologies, and I suddenly realized that actually I really didn't understand social media. And so I decided to at least make an effort. I emailed my colleague Professor Brown and I said, "I'm thinking of blogging, what do you think?" And he was very helpful, came back, gave me some tips and hints on how to go about blogging, to have a number of topics on the go, to follow key people and that kind of thing, and then think about the things to blog about. So, blogging has become an absolute central part of what I do, from working up ideas which then might become papers or book chapters, through to summarizing things at a conference or a keynote I've done, through to summarizing key resources … just a whole range of different things. And I find it very motivational because people give you comments back. They say, "I like this. I don't like that," so it's just fantastic. It's just really, really great. I've been blogging since 2007, and I was lucky. My first blog post was picked up by a well known person in the field who I didn't know personally at the time, but I knew of, of course. And he shared my post and said, "Oh, I've just found this really interesting new post," and loads of new people started following me. So, blogging's become central … In fact I'm doing a keynote on Thursday and I've just done a blog post about it, provided a link to the paper, and so on.

As far as Facebook is concerned, I was in for a while before it really connected with me, but now it's absolutely central to what I do …

Interviewer: To your work as well?

Anna: Absolutely … And I just find it amazing, the kind of things you find, and always when I'm just about to do a keynote, I'm trying to think of some new, fresh angles, and invariably there are two or three things coming through on Facebook or Twitter that you can build into them. I also use Skype. A very good friend and colleague isn't on social media, but we Skype a lot. So we Skype chat probably two or three times a week. So I do do chatting with Skype.

And, going back to social media, it's both a mixture of silly trivial stuff and pictures of cats and food, and serious stuff. So, it's half and half. Twitter is probably more professional. But I like the mix in Facebook, and I love the serendipity of connections. I've just literally, just before meeting with you, found a blog post about 13 ways technology will revolutionize education in the next few years, and I thought, "Oh great, I can use that in my keynote on Thursday."

These tools help me keep in touch with people. There is a guy I didn't really know very well when I was at Anonymous University and for some reason he kind of chats lots every now and again, and we will say things like, "Oh, I am sorry to hear about such and such," or, "How is the new job going". So sometimes I am surprised by the people who connect with you.

The other thing I love about social media is the way in which they are a leveller. There is no longer a hierarchy, whereas in the past somebody wouldn't have nerves, as a student for example, to maybe email me. PhD students, researchers will connect online on Facebook or Twitter, and then they'll send a little chat and say, "Oh, these are my research questions, what do you think", or, "Have you got any links to the elite papers?" And it is just great to be able to provide that connection and support. I think that's incredibly valuable.

Interviewer: Right.

Anna: So that's been fantastic. And both with Twitter and Facebook, what I find amazing is the number of people I've become friends with, genuine friends with, that I've then met face-to-face. So for example, although we've never met, I feel as if I already know lots about you, and there's so many other people I've met.

A girl once came up to me at a conference, no it wasn't a conference, it was a meeting in Paris, and she was quite a bubbly girl with big, fuzzy, black hair, and she bounced up to me and she said, "Hi, I'm Shakira!" And I thought, "Oh, who's this?" And then, she said, "I'm @Username!" And I went, "Oh, @Username!" So, it's been amazing.

There was a guy in Spain who I met at a conference. He came across a conference lobby hall to me and said hello … and then a few months later, I'm doing a PhD examination for him and then I'm having a glass of wine outside a cafe with him.

So, I've got countless stories of how I've connected with people through social media. And I just love the serendipity of it. I love the way in which people share. I think it's very important that social media is a two-way relationship, so you have to give as much as you take, that's a really key element. And I think each of us develops our own personal identity or persona in these online spaces. So obviously, I think because of the nationwide work I do and my personality, I'm very, very open in social media, always.

For some people, being too open is maybe a bit risky and uncomfortable but for me it's just the way I do things so that's fine. So, I think social media

has become important for me both professionally and personally. I've also got a personal blog, which is about cooking and travel, two things I really love. And I was once at a conference in Berlin, and the woman who organized it, came up to me, gave me a big hug, and said, "I just love your food posts."
[chuckle]

Interviewer: That's great. I want to learn more about you and the people you connect to. When you're online, do the people you connect with belong to one group or multiple groups? And if multiple, what are those groups?

Anna: Multiple groups, and I see social media as a kind of onion layering. So there are certain people I interact with a lot. Both professionally and personally. So I had a colleague for example, and he's quite a character, somebody who I didn't really know very well personally and I actually got to know him, not personally face-to-face, but through his great sense of humour online. He's always taking a nicky at me, commenting on my posts and stuff like that.

And so there will be certain people I know will comment on things or will retweet. This guy in Spain always retweets anything I write … And some people are people that I'll have lots of banter with. There's a woman whom I've never met, she's a cousin of somebody else's who's connected with me and she's always commenting on food posts. So I posted a picture of a dish I made, and she says, "It looks like a dog's dinner" And I said, "Oh you seem to be having peas again!"
[chuckle]

Other people are more serious; A colleague texted me before and said, "I love your tweets, you provide a wealth of knowledge, it's very generous … but I just zone out when you talk about personal stuff." And yet I've connected with his wife and have great banter with her. So it's a mixture. And sometimes I'm really surprised by who knows who. Gosh, I didn't know so-and-so knew them. How do they knew them? But that happens often.

Interviewer: Sometimes that happens for me even years down the road. I've been talking to people who I think are from totally, totally separate parts of my networks and then I realize there's an intersection there. So, you were saying that some people you interact with are only interested in one facet what you're presenting. Is that …

Anna: Yeah, yeah. Certain people will only be interested in my professional blogs or posts about things. Certain people are interested in conferences, it's a complete mix and it's a complete network and I think it's an interesting way to see the connection of personal and professional. My sister has recently got into Facebook only because her daughter had a baby boy, so suddenly now *she's* on Facebook posting pictures of her grandson and as a result she starts to get more into social media. But the interesting thing is, some of my closest friends are not on social media. So my best friend works for [company], and she's in security, and she won't touch social media with a large pole. So I think it's quite interesting. Likewise my best friend from school is not on there.

Interviewer: You've been pretty clear that you present both the personal and professional online. How do you think that the people that you connect with would describe you?

Anna: I do sometimes wonder about that … whether my open style is offensive to some people or too open or too personal. Some people may think that [certain aspects of my blogging are] inappropriate. Pretty much all aspects of my life are open, but then again I do distinguish between what to share and not share. I mean, some people I think are too open and they'll post, "I'm really depressed today," or, "Having another bottle of wine," or something like that. There's a girl I connect with and I'm quite uncomfortable with her, I should really de-friend her. She's from high school and I don't remember her that well, and she's always posting kind of quite negative things; she's drinking lots and on Wednesday she kept posting pictures of me and tagging me on Facebook when I was 15. And believe me, at 15, I wasn't a pretty sight.

It is true, though, that occasionally we all make faux pas on social media. A colleague of mine went to a conference a couple of years ago, met up with friends a few days before, and posted about it on Facebook. I said, "Well off for another jolly" or something, you know, totally lighthearted. And he texted me immediately and said, "That's really inappropriate. You know I'm on Facebook with some of my bosses." And I thought "Gosh, he's right. I shouldn't have said that." And I immediately apologized and immediately took it down. But on the whole, I don't think I've been too bad. As I said earlier, I think some people are, "Got a mega hangover this morning," or "Calling in sick," and all these kinds of things, and you think, "That's not good."

[laughter]

To get back to your question, I think most people would describe me as open with a reasonable sense of humour, willing to share, generous in terms of time. But as I said, for some people it may be that I'm too open … but you can't change the way you are.

Interviewer: I think that actually you've touched on a piece that's important. There's the personal/professional access, right, which you have both online, but then there's also the public/private access, and even though you are personal as you've shared, the way that your acquaintance shares sort of *morose* postings, is obviously different. I'm assuming we all have those feelings, but some of us don't express them publicly. Because there is a lot there, and you are open and generous with a lot of things, this doesn't necessarily indicate, I am assuming, that you are generous with everything, that every thought that goes through your head appears online.

Anna: No, not everything. And it is interesting, it's been quite a tough year for a number of reasons. My daughter's dad died unexpectedly and I didn't post anything about that. If you were to look back on my Facebook profile, you wouldn't see anything. Although, if you knew me well enough, you could probably read between the lines. I wasn't being so humorous online, I was perhaps quieter than normal. ... A colleague once said that he found it intrusive that when he was in a down period, suddenly people were contacting him and asking "what's wrong," and he found that to be an intrusion of his privacy. ... So it is interesting. And people *can* be intrusive in this way. I don't know if you've had it. I have had a few strange experiences recently on Facebook where people have sent me an invitation request, and normally I will accept if they're friends of friends, or if it's clear that they're working in the same area. But then I look at these guys, and it is always guys, and I can't see any connection, and maybe they have just been bored, and you think, "That's just odd."

I don't connect with people like that. A few people I have connected with, and then suddenly they are bombarding me with chat messages, and saying, "Oh thank you for accepting my invitation, how are you madam. ... "

Interviewer: You're like, "Hush now."

Anna: Yeah, exactly.

Interviewer: Anna, how has your use of social media changed over time? Since you really got on Twitter and Facebook, do you see a general transition that's happening in any direction, or are you largely using it more or less the same?

Anna: It's become more and more embedded in everything I do. With Twitter, I was lucky, because the university I was at at the time, lots of other people got on Twitter at the same time, so I had an immediate network very quickly. And, as I said, it took a little bit longer for me to get into Facebook, but, I mean, I look at Facebook and Twitter all day, because I will look at them and keep up to date with them, and reply to comments and stuff.

Interviewer: Was there any one memorable response that stood out for you on social media?

Anna: I think there have been lots actually. … So when I got a new job, a lot of people made nice comments and stuff like that. When I finished my book, it was great, the kind of comments people put, 'cause a bit like your PhD, it felt like my PhD in the area, it was a lot of work, a labor of love. And it was just lovely when people said, "Oh I really like that. And thanks for that."

Interviewer: Okay, last couple of questions. This one goes up sort of 10,000 feet from your own personal experience to your analysis of the space. What boundaries do you see around what is speakable, or disclosable online? And what gaps do you see around what we don't share or talk about? If any.

Anna: I think you have to be very careful what you share online. I think it goes back again to each person's individual identity. Some people love blogging, some people hate it. I think … the boundaries of things … inappropriate comments, sexist comments, racist comments, I think are out of scope. Politics is interesting, isn't it? Kind of boundary one. But it depends on what you write about the political aspects, I guess.

But I think disclosing too much might make others feel uncomfortable, or be a burden in some way to people. But I think most people, most I'd say, are fairly digitally literate if you like, in terms of how to use these spaces appropriately. Well, I guess the people in our field are. But it's interesting I was commenting to someone the other day, I think 99% of the people I'm connected with online are on the left political persuasion. But I guess that's not surprising because I work in academia.

So if I was in some other field I guess it might be different. But it is an interesting mix of professional people, family, friends, and how they kind of interact or don't interact really. I think again it goes back to personal preferences. I think it's really what each of us feel comfortable about sharing, what's appropriate for us and what's appropriate for our network. I mean we connect with people, we're friends with people because we like them, we have shared interests, context, humour. I mean it's exactly the same in the online space. I don't view it as any different really.

Interviewer: I understand. That's great, is there anything else that you want to tell me about your experiences on social media?

Anna: No, I think that's probably fairly well covered it. I think the benefits definitely outweigh the disadvantages for me. People say, "How do you find the time?" You find the time because it's useful, motivational, and adds value in some ways.

Interviewer: Okay. That's wonderful. Thank you so much for taking the time to talk to me about that. That was really helpful.

4

NETWORKS OF KNOWLEDGE CREATION AND DISSEMINATION

How are scholars using online networks to engage in the creation and dissemination of knowledge? What scholarly materials do they post online? What scholarly activities are they engaged in? In this chapter, I explore the milieu that scholars enact online with respect to knowledge creation and dissemination, and describe how academics use networks for scholarship. I present examples of academics using networks to support each others' scholarly endeavours, to conduct research, and to share their knowledge with communities outside of academia.

The image of the "lone scholar" tirelessly working on his or her research in a dimly lit office is in stark contrast to the connected and visible scholarly activities that scholars engage in online, at least by the measure of the scholars that I have encountered in my investigation of networked scholarship. While a number of specialized tools have been developed specifically for networked scholarly practice (e.g., Mendeley; see Figure 4.1 for Academia.edu), scholars also use their own individual websites, most often blogs, as spaces in which they enact and pursue their scholarship in a visible manner. Personal websites often serve as areas where faculty's digital presence is aggregated and various scholarly artifacts are featured. For example, the personal websites of those who actively manage their online presence frequently feature the creator's blog, Twitter feed, teaching/research statements, scholarly artifacts (e.g., copies of syllabi and publications), and links to topics of interest (e.g., professional organizations) or blogs that the individual reads.

FIGURE 4.1 Screenshot of Academia.edu

Digital Residents vs. Digital Visitors

Not all scholars use digital technologies and social media in the same ways, of course. While some members of a university community may be deeply professionally embedded in online platforms and networks, others may approach digital practices far more cautiously, or with instrumental rather than social purposes in mind. One way to conceptualize the differences between scholars who fully embrace social media vis-a-vis those whose approach may preclude them from taking full advantage of networked platforms is to consider the purposes and perspectives they bring to their engagement.

White and LeCornu (2011) use the continuum of digital visitors and digital residents to understand participation in online spaces. Applied to networked participatory scholarship, digital residents are those scholars who understand the affordances of the participatory web for scholarship, cultivate digital identities and relationships online, and view the web as a crucial component of their scholarly work and identity. Digital visitors on the other hand are those scholars who use the web as a tool when they see a need for it. A digital visitor would visit electronic databases to update a literature review for a paper when a need arises, while digital residents would have developed a learning network of colleagues through which they could track and categorize publications and resources of interest on an ongoing basis. Other than using tools for information management, being a digital resident also means cultivating an online identity – not just having a presence online via a website, but actively managing that presence. For instance, remaining visible on a social networking and fast-moving platform such as Twitter means that one has to share often and frequently, or else one's voice and presence are diluted in the sea of information that is already present. Coupling these issues with other activities that demand scholars' time – activities that may be more highly rewarded in the current academic structure – and it becomes clear why online participation akin to digital resident status may not represent all of today's scholars.

Practices: What Residents Do

In one of my own research projects, I dedicated time to be an active participant and contributor on social media sites, collecting data via ethnographic means. In these spaces, I interacted with educators, researchers, and students within the field of Educational Technology, participated in virtual events (e.g., open courses), and kept a journal of these activities. This journal consisted of observations, thoughts, reflections, and a number of digital artifacts (e.g., screenshots, hyperlinks, news articles). Some of these artifacts were derived from a wide array of social media sites such as blogs, micro-blogging sites, and video-sharing sites. This journal centred on three main questions, "What am I observing in my social media participation with regard to scholarly practice? What phenomena and/or issues arise? What do these observations mean for scholarly practice, and how can we make sense of them?" Some of the main practices that I observed scholars enacting in public digital spaces were the following:

- Announcing publications, awards, and job opportunities, among other things
- Sharing drafts of manuscripts and requesting/receiving feedback on them
- Developing and releasing textbooks written as part of a course (e.g., Amado et al, 2011; Correia, 2012)
- Sharing syllabi and instructional activities
- Live-streaming or sharing video/photographs from one's own teaching
- Live-blogging and live-tweeting a conference keynote or session
- Authoring and participating in the writing of collaborative documents pertaining to conference sessions/workshops
- Engaging in debates and commentary on professional issues
- Teaching: for example, scholars have led open courses which invite participation from individuals who are not formally enrolled at the institution in which the course is offered (e.g., Hilton et al., 2010)
- Making one's tenure and promotion materials publicly available
- Reflecting on and conversing about the doctoral process and thesis/dissertation

- – doctoral students using blogs and wikis to share their work, and to reflect upon and document their progress
- – self-organized systems through which some of these activities are enacted have also been formed (e.g., #PhDChat – see page 43)
- Creating video trailers to describe, promote, and highlight academic artifacts (e.g., books)
- Crowdsourcing and help-seeking with professional activities (e.g., research, teaching): individuals ask for help in locating research literature or relevant materials

Research on the extent to which these practices are present is scarce, though large-scale social media surveys of US faculty show (a) increasing adoption of social media tools for professional purposes over the years, (b) greater use of social media for personal rather than professional purposes, and (c) around half of faculty members using social media for professional purposes (Moran, Seaman, & Tinti-Kane, 2011; Moran & Tinti-Kane, 2013).

Use of particular tools undoubtedly varies among scholars. While Bowman's research shows that social media uptake by faculty members ranges from 70 percent (Facebook) to 50 percent (Google Plus), a survey of 1,600 education scholars by researchers at Michigan State University (Bergland, 2014) puts the use of social media for professional purposes at much lower rates for Twitter (15 percent), YouTube (28 percent) and Facebook (39 percent).

Further, the ways that adopters use social media tools also varies. Bowman's (2015) survey of 613 scholars who indicated having a Twitter account, showed that 42 percent of respondents reported using Twitter for both personal and professional purposes, while use of Twitter for distinctly personal and distinctly professional purposes was less prevalent (29 percent for each use). For instance, social media has been found to both permeate some scholars' lives and to have been used in targeted goal-oriented ways (Kieslinger, 2015).

In the cases where scholars use social media for knowledge creation and dissemination purposes, we observe a diverse range of practices to support such goals.

Timothy Gowers, a professor at the University of Cambridge at the time, used his blog as a platform to engage individuals in producing ideas and solutions to a complex mathematical problem, generating substantial contributions from 27 individuals, and announcing a proof of the problem approximately a month and a half after the inception of the project (Gowers & Nielsen, 2009).

Alec Couros, a professor at the University of Regina, taught an online course in fall 2010 entitled "Social Media and Open Education" that was available to anyone for free. Couros asked colleagues to help him in teaching the 345 students who expressed interest in enrolling as non-credit students. Couros' volunteer colleagues acted as online network mentors and actively supported these students. Within a few days, 124 individuals volunteered to serve as mentors and collectively aided Couros in teaching the course (A. Couros, personal communication, June 13, 2011).

Results from a research project I conducted to understand what scholars do on Twitter may further illuminate these activities. In that project, I collected the latest 100 public tweets from 45 early adopters of Twitter who represented multiple academic disciplines. Thirty-eight were men and seven were women. Two scholars did not list their location, and the rest were located in the United States (32), Canada (6), UK (2), Spain (2), and Portugal (1). I categorized their tweets to understand what they were doing on Twitter.

One of the findings was that scholars used their Twitter network to intentionally enhance their own knowledge and practice. For instance, participants requested examples and resources that they could use in their teaching (e.g., "Do you have any excellent examples of interactive whiteboard uses in education? I'm looking for examples for Thursday's class," and "Can you point me to your favorite politicians' Facebook pages that I can use in my course?"). In other instances, instructors sought recommendations and assistance that would enhance their skills and/or practice (e.g., "How do you use [technology] in or out of the classroom? I want to learn from you, so please tell me about it" or "[Software] does not allow me to create an interactive image to publish on the Web. What software can do this?"). Finally, participants sought information relevant to their scholarship and research (e.g., "I am writing a paper on [topic]. If you have knowledge of [topic] I would be grateful for your suggestions," and "Does anyone have any article recommendations on the impact of Internet access on [population of interest]?").

In addition to requests for assistance and input, I observed the responses from the community to such requests. For instance, participants answered questions (e.g., "Yes, @user. [School name] should add a class on [topic]" or "@user1 @user2, here is the information on [topic]: [URL]"), and provided resources in response to such requests (e.g., "This is an example of digital content creation: [URL], @user"). In other cases, participants directed users to examples and offered to provide further input if that was needed (e.g., "Here is an example [URL] @user. I can also send my course schedule if you need it"), or voluntarily offered suggestions to colleagues: "If you teach [topic], this might be valuable to your students: [URL]."

It is important to realize however that knowledge creation and dissemination practices, as well as requests for scholarly assistance as we see above, vary from platform to platform. Social media sites have their own norms and structures. What researchers observe in one platform (e.g., Facebook) may not transfer to other platforms (e.g., Twitter or Pinterest). This poses challenges for the generalizability of results that researchers may observe when they examine scholars' participation on social media (cf. Tufekci, 2014). Thus, the help-seeking behaviours I found on Twitter, may not fully transfer to help-seeking behaviours on Facebook, even though researchers have observed help-seeking behaviours on Facebook as well.

While such behaviours may not be exactly the same, what might be some common elements? Tufekci's argument is convincing in that practices may differ between social media platforms (and that big data analyses focusing on one platform may not transfer to others). However, one common element in the use of social media for knowledge production and dissemination that seems to be a persistent theme is the concept of *crowdsourcing*. Crowdsourcing refers to the process of gathering contributions from large groups of individuals in order to solve a common problem or tackle a challenge. Though readers may be familiar with modern crowdsourcing examples that are mediated by technology (e.g., Wikipedia as a content crowdsourcing platform), the practice existed long before the rise of social media. For instance, the design of the Sydney Opera House was crowdsourced. It was based on a 1955 international design competition that received 233 entries. Crowdsourcing content and ideas characterizes social media use, and scholars have capitalized on this practice to gather readings for their syllabi, activities for their courses, resources for their research, and other input – including effort – intended to solve scholarly problems. One aspect of knowledge creation and dissemination in which crowdsourcing activities have been conducted that makes for an interesting phenomenon is the sharing of scholarly papers.

Sharing Scholarly Papers

Imagine being at a university whose library does not have access to a journal that you need for your teaching or research. Or that even though you have access to the journal, the year in which a particular paper was published falls outside of your institution's subscription dates. For example, the journal may impose a 6-month lag between the time the paper is published and the time it becomes available electronically. Or, as I discovered, you may request an article via interlibrary loan and licensing restrictions may only allow you to receive the paper in hard copy. What options are available to you?

You could purchase the article. Or, you could email the article's author and ask for a copy of the paper. Alternatively, you could search for the article online in the hopes that the author has self-archived the paper (e.g., on his/her personal website or institutional repository).

Scholars may seek the assistance of their networks to access scholarly papers that they need, posting requests on Twitter or Facebook. "Does anyone have access to a digital copy of 'Networked Scholars' by Veletsianos to share?" may be the type of request that I might come across in the future. In response to similar requests, I have observed academics reply with Dropbox links to papers (Figure 4.2) or with confirmations that they would provide papers via email.

Reminiscent of peer-to-peer networks for music sharing, scholars have sought the assistance of broader networks of individuals and have used PirateUniversity. org, ThePaperBay.com, and the Scholar subreddit to access scholarship that they need. On these websites, individuals request papers that they do not have access to, and those who have access (e.g., through their institution's libraries) provide them with a copy of the papers. The Scholar subreddit for example has more than

Tunks – 2012 – (Done) An Introduction an...nline Instruction with Web 2 . 0 Tools.pdf	May 23, 2013, 12:47 AM	112 KB	Adobe...ument
Ivala, Gachago – 2012 – (Done) Social me...and blogs at a University of technology.pdf	May 23, 2013, 12:47 AM	1.3 MB	Adobe...ument
Fisher, Baird – 2005 – (Done) Online learn...upport, self–regulation, and retention.pdf	May 23, 2013, 12:47 AM	217 KB	Adobe...ument
Allen – 2012 – (Done) An education in Facebook.pdf	May 23, 2013, 12:47 AM	545 KB	Adobe...ument
Vesisenaho, Valtonen – 2010 – (Done) Ble...tivate Students' Collaborative Learning.pdf	May 23, 2013, 12:47 AM	247 KB	Adobe...ument
Junco, Elavsky, Heiberger – 2013 – (Done)...ollaboration, engagement and success.pdf	May 23, 2013, 12:46 AM	681 KB	Adobe...ument

FIGURE 4.2 Sharing of Dropbox Links to Papers

24,000 subscribers at the time of writing. Reddit.com is a popular content aggregator whose content was contributed by users. A subreddit is a community of users who share a common interest (e.g., exercise, veganism, education). The Scholar subreddit is described as a place for "requesting and sharing specific articles available in various databases" and advises individuals to "be aware of copyright issues and Fair Use Copyright," while cautioning them that "many journal sources embed identifying information into the PDF."

The #ICanHazPdf hashtag is another way that users have accessed papers that they need. This works as follows: a user posts a note on Twitter describing the paper that they need access to (e.g., title and author information or DOI) and includes the #ICanHazPdf hashtag with it. Users who follow the hashtag and who are willing and able to provide access to the paper locate the paper and make it available for download. They notify the original sender and once the original sender retrieves it, the tweets pertaining to this transaction are often erased.

These activities are important because they suggest that individuals are willing and able to circumvent and defy restrictions to the sharing of knowledge and research. In fact, in my ethnographic investigations, I found that broadening access to scholarship appears to be close to the hearts and minds of many scholars who use the Internet for professional purposes. Even though some may not publicly embrace or endorse the activities described above, they often make their stance in support of open access known. For example, a number of them have blogged their refusal to publish in or review for non–Open Access journals.

Illustrative Examples

There are different ways that scholars have used social media and online networks to create and share knowledge. Here are four in-depth examples.

Example #1: Colleagues Helping Colleagues on Facebook

My colleagues and I recently completed a synthesis of the literature on a topic of interest. We identified about two hundred papers on the topic, and as we were examining this literature, we became interested in exploring whether the authors contributing to this literature came from different disciplines. We searched the literature for ideas on how other researchers studied the presence of interdisciplinarity in a corpus of papers, and it seemed that one popular approach was to categorize authors by the discipline of their doctoral program and report descriptive statistics. We sought to complement our findings by asking colleagues on social media for their input. If someone used any of the methods we found, s/he might be able to give us more input as to their relative merits.

I posted the following note, presented here verbatim, on the "Professors of Instructional Design and Technology" group on Facebook:

> Does anyone know how I can go about examining whether there's evidence of interdisciplinarity in a set of papers? For example, let's say that I collected 100 papers examining learning experiences in online courses. What are some ways to use that would enable me to say that there is or that there is no evidence of interdisciplinarity in my data corpus of 100 papers? I could categorize authors by discipline, and can report if there are collaborations between authors from different disciplines, but that's as far as I got. Any thoughts?

A number of colleagues provided suggestions. Wendy Gentry was one of the individuals who replied. At the time of writing, Wendy was a doctoral student at Virginia Tech. She offered these thoughts, and gave me permission to reproduce them here:

> Something to ponder:
> 1. Categorize the citations within the papers by discipline.
> 2. Identify and categorize any referenced theories by founding discipline (multi-step citation trail backward in time).
> 3. Categorize the authors by discipline of their PhD (multi-step search in vitas, bios, back flaps of any authored books).
> 4. Or, flip the concept by going forward in time and identifying the disciplines where the papers are cited.

Given Wendy's familiarity with the topic, I asked if she knew of any papers that used any of these approaches, so that we could see them in practice. She replied:

> You may regret asking … but here are some places to start!

Wendy then recommended a key foundational text as a point of departure, and offered an in-depth analysis of five alternative options for assessing cross-disciplinarity: interdisciplinarity by citations received (import of knowledge), discipline of PhD, interdisciplinarity by exported citations, Aboela's (2007) research into interdisciplinarity, and her own personal co-citation techniques and steps. Her response was extensive and thoroughly cited, and graciously offered a synthesis of the field.

Wendy's reply illustrated the depth of knowledge exchange and serious academic discourse that can occur on social networks. While one would expect this exchange to happen in a doctoral defense, scholarly presentation, or in private among colleagues, this example is neither original, nor uncommon.

Example #2: #PhDChat

Social media messages often include hashtags. A hashtag refers to the use of a # symbol followed by a word or a phrase (e.g., #education, #elections2016, #TechConference15). The practice originated on Twitter and has spread to other platforms. Each hashtag collates all contributions on a particular topic. Hashtags enable users to group and retrieve messages around a common topic or event; this practice has allowed users to form networks around shared interests and practices. One hashtag network that my colleagues and I have examined is #PhDChat (Ford, Veletsianos, & Resta, 2014). This network arose when a group of UK doctoral students began using it in 2010 to hold discussions related to pursuing a doctoral degree (Thackray, n.d.). Individuals convened weekly to discuss specified topics and over time, #PhDChat's membership grew. Individuals often use the network to update each other on their progress, share resources,

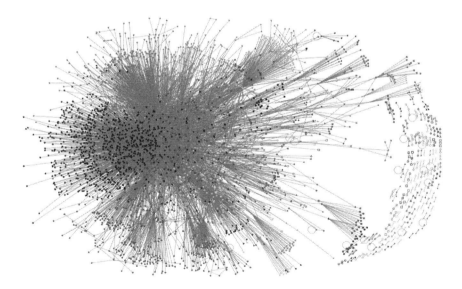

FIGURE 4.3 Visualization of the Network Of Users Who Mentioned or Were Mentioned in a Tweet Containing the #PhDChat Hashtag

learn about the profession, socialize, and provide emotional and academic support to each other. Figure 4.3 shows a visualization of the network of users who mentioned or were mentioned in a tweet containing the #PhDChat hashtag. This image shows that some users comprise the core group of participants while others had little interactions with the group.

Example #3: Identifying Fish Specimens

In 2011, a team of ichthyologists set out to examine the species of fish in Guyana's Cuyuni River. They collected 5,000 fish specimens, but in order to leave the country they needed to report species counts to the Guyanese government. The researchers explained: "As a condition to securing an export permit, we had just one week to complete a detailed report with each of our 5,000 specimens identified to genus and species. Given the limited library resources at our disposal and the time constraint, the task seemed impossible" (Sidlauskas et al., 2011, p. 537). One of the scholars on the team, Devin Bloom, a doctoral student, suggested that they post the photos on Facebook and call on their colleagues to identify the samples they collected. The team had already taken photos of each fish and by uploading the photos (that is, their data) to Facebook, their contacts, (the majority of whom held doctorates in ichthyology-related fields) could help them identify the species. And it worked. Their networks helped them identify more than 90% of the 5,000 fish specimens collected within 24 hours. The researchers were appreciative:

> We packed our specimens for shipment and returned home, grateful beyond words for the generosity of our colleagues, and for the social network that allowed us to harness their vast collective expertise and provide faster and more accurate identifications than we ever would have dreamed possible.
>
> *(Sidlauskas et al., 2011, p. 537)*

Example #4: Reddit "Ask Me Anything" Threads

I have mentioned Reddit.com as a popular content aggregator and the existence of various communities within the site, called subreddits. One subreddit is called IAmA, which stands for "I am A." In this community, users post "Ask Me Anything" or "Ask Me Almost/Absolutely Anything" threads, inviting others to ask questions of them. For example, a user might post a thread as follows: I am a researcher specializing in educational technology. Ask Me Anything about how people learn with technology. This community is one of the most popular on the site, and it features more than 8 million subscribers. "Ask me Anything" threads appear in other subreddits as well (e.g., in the Science subreddit).

While politicians, actors, and artists have used this platform, a number of scholars have also initiated threads and have sought to share their knowledge with this community. Such scholars included Tina Seelig[1] (a professor of Innovation and Creativity at Stanford), Steven D. Munger[2] (a researcher of tastes and odours at the University of Florida), Peggy Mason[3] (a professor of Neurobiology at the University of Chicago who studies empathy in rats), David Kimhy[4] (a professor of Psychiatry at the University of Columbia who discussed the results of his latest research study), and Mae Jemison[5] (former NASA astronaut who discussed the teaching and learning of science).

Owens (2014) provides more history on this phenomenon and describes in more detail how, through these threads, "Reddit created the world's largest dialogue between scientists and the general public." However, it is important to note that Reddit's creators impose little restrictions and take a hands-off approach to user-contributed content. Thus, while Reddit features some shining examples of knowledge exchange, it has often – and rightly so – been criticized for being a festering ground for communities promoting misogyny, racism, and homophobia.

Conclusion

Online social networks offer much hope for improving and rethinking scholarly communities. Central to this hope is the idea of crowdsourcing, but also the generosity and goodwill of colleagues. While collegiality may be a characteristic of scholarly networks, tensions, conflict and conundrums also permeate these spaces. We explore these topics next by examining the complicated realities that an individual scholar faces when considering the use of social media.

Notes

1   www.reddit.com/r/IAmA/comments/383mpu/i_teach_creativity_and_innovation_
    at_stanford_i
2   www.reddit.com/r/science/comments/3456kh/hello_my_name_is_steven_d_munger_
    and_i_am_the
3   www.reddit.com/r/science/comments/23o5w4/science_ama_series_hi_im_peggy_
    mason_i_study
4   www.reddit.com/r/science/comments/31v3mx/science_ama_series_im_dr_david_kimhy_
    of_columbia
5   www.reddit.com/r/science/comments/2x0i75/science_ama_series_ask_me_anything_
    about_learning

5

JAIME: THE COMPLICATED REALITIES OF DAY-TO-DAY SOCIAL MEDIA USE

Jaime is an assistant professor at a large research-focused university in the United States who is quite comfortable with technology. Jaime doesn't see technology as a barrier to teaching/research and often experiments with technology and tries "just about everything."

Jaime however, has more social and ethical questions about technology than technical ones, and is ambivalent about social media, especially as they pertain to collapsing contexts and bringing together individuals who may not fully represent Jaime's identity or perspectives.

Jaime's feelings are shared by the majority of the scholars I have interacted with and/or interviewed. Thus, I'm sharing Jaime's story here because this narrative represents the "most-likely" case of a scholar using social media. While Jaime's concerns may not be shared by everyone, they are shared by many, regardless of gender.

I have structured Jaime's report as a first-person narrative. Imagine Jaime reflecting on social media and networked practice, as many of us have done, after yet another case of social media turbulence hits the news:

> Facebook is probably the only social media tool that I use. I mean, I have Twitter and have followed people, but I don't really care for it that much. If someone asked me what social media I use, I would have to say Facebook. I post status updates and sometimes these are related to things that are happening at the university. Sometimes they are not. They might be generic posts like "hey, do people know about the rally that's coming up on Monday?" and sometimes I might post something more specific like: "oh, this really

cool thing just happened in my class" or "with this student I'm tutoring." So sometimes it's just things like that, and sometimes it's related to news items around education or anything that's happening that I kind of want to give a shout-out to or post a link. Sometimes it's articles or a book that comes out. I also ask people for recommendations about certain topics. If I know I'm going to teach something and I really need a book looking at a topic, I would put that out there and ask whether anyone had any recommendations. So it's really a way to gather information as much as it is to share information.

I remember a time when I used to get up in the morning, and check email and then check Facebook. And then it flipped. I would get up in the morning and check Facebook and then check email. But the good thing I liked about doing Facebook first sometimes and, especially when there's a lot going on in politics, folks on the East coast who were up before me would already have links to op-eds in the *New York Times* or stuff in the *Huffington Post*. So I would get up and be like, "oh I need to read this and read this and read this," and so for me it was really great, because it kind of pulled out the things that I would be interested in looking at that I might not have looked at before.

I've also used things in my courses, and I really feel like I've learned a lot professionally. For example, one time someone posted about a book, maybe two weeks ago, and I ordered it and can't wait to read it. But if I relied on myself to look through our profession's organization's catalogue, I would never have found the book.

I've never done video posts on Facebook, so I've never used that tool before, and I'm sure there's lots of other options on Facebook that I don't even know about.

One of the first social media sites I used was MySpace. I didn't look at that as a professional space at all. It was really just a fun place, a place where everything didn't need to be about teaching and research. I needed a space to just be me and that's what that space was. I didn't want it to morph into anything else. I think MySpace allowed me to connect with people that I didn't really have a lot of time to sit and talk on the phone with, that I wasn't going to write letters with, I probably wasn't going to visit a lot, but it allowed me to say, "hey, this is what's going on in my life, these are the books I'm reading, these are the stores I want to shop at, these are like vacations I want to take." It was just "who wants to go to Miami for the weekend?" It wasn't a space to share photos that my family and I took at our picnic or what my class did.

It was literally a space about me, a space to kind of claim for myself and not have all of these other things encroach on it. I guess in some way I kind of felt that MySpace was just a place to reconnect with the things that I like to do and the people that I want to talk to and only make that circle of friends as big or as small as I want it to be.

I then started using Facebook. I don't think there was anything negative about MySpace. ... It may have just been "oh, people aren't using MySpace anymore, everyone's on Facebook." And I use Facebook in a different way. Facebook was strictly about connecting with folks in different universities that I had met at conferences and *then it kind of morphed into lots of stuff: a little professional, a little catch up with family, a little catch up with friends, and a little just to find out what's going on.* It started out as professional and then became more personal. (emphasis added)

People who weren't so much folks in the academy that I wanted to connect with or colleagues or friends that I had worked with in other situations, people on the periphery of my profession or even people on an outer circle would start to request me as a friend and *it became an interesting political thing to try and figure out who I accepted and who I did not accept.* I think that is a generational thing because I know younger kids accept everybody and they have like 5,000 friends or whatever (laughs; emphasis added)

But, for me, it became something bigger. Gosh, if I'm using this to network and I haven't talked to some people in fifteen years, I don't really know who they are anymore and what if they write something that's not appropriate?

I felt that I was beginning to censor myself and I resented the fact that I had to censor who was on my page or had access to it. This was before all of these personal controls were available so that was tough. I ended up doing much less posting – sometimes none at all – because I was really not sure what my posts would mean to people. And I had former students on there and so it just became an exercise in navigating the politics of Facebook, which is something I hadn't thought about at all.

Since then I've gotten really good at ignoring friend requests or at sending notes to people and saying:

> I'm really glad that you reached out! I know you were a student of mine when you were in second grade or you were a parent of mine when your kid was in second grade but this is a space that is a professional space or for family.

I've tried to find ways to either respond to someone so it doesn't feel like I am just completely ignoring them ... or, completely ignore them and be okay with it.

But, I didn't like the fact that I was putting so much thought into it. I didn't like that I had to sit down and figure out who to accept and how to respond to them if I decided not to accept them as "friends."

I ended up creating all of these silly rules to decide whether to accept or reject friend requests. If students were in college, I'd accept them. But, I don't want a high school kid, even if they were in my class when they were nine, having access to my life, because there are adults on Facebook and sometimes they'll post links to different articles or it could just be that there are political conversations that are happening and I just don't know how this kid who is fifteen will respond if they have access to post something to my page. So it really became: "how much of my life do I want to share with this person?"

With the controls provided to me by Facebook, I can say, "well, I'll accept so-and-so but I won't let them see or do any of these things." This whole process makes me wish that I would have just created an account and only kept it for professional networking because I wouldn't have had any of these issues to deal with. So I think that I created the conundrum that I live in now.

What do I do with this tool, since it's taken on kind of a different spin?

I mean there's a lot of personal and professional things on there. I am visiting a friend in a week, and she messaged me on Facebook: "That movie we wanted to see isn't going to be playing when you come up here, so do you want to see something else?" So, it still has this like "are we going shopping here or what?" That feel is still there. But it also has a "are you gonna co-author this piece with me" or "did you see this piece that just came out in this journal" kind of feel.

And it seems that the connections I have are colleagues, friends, some former students, whereas in MySpace it was very different. And more family, too, I guess I forgot about family but yeah there's family on Facebook that I don't think I had at all when I was on MySpace. I don't think any of my family was there at all, it was really just friends.

From all these people, I think there's just a core group of people that really are the folks that I communicate with and then there's other people that I don't even know how they come to see my status update. So, I don't know how that's filtered. How do Facebook's algorithms determine whose updates you get to see or not see? How does Facebook determine who to show my updates to? So, I think the more you follow people the more they end up showing in my feed ... so it starts to become a smaller, smaller circle.

I posted a link to an interview recently and some people liked it and commented on it, and a conversation sort of started after that. Well, some of them were faculty here, and some of them were people from back home and some of them were people that I went to church with and so this thing kind of took on a life of its own.

I was thinking, "oh my gosh I haven't heard from you in forever … why are you even … why do you even have something to say about this?" I didn't like it at all, because it was … it's difficult to explain … it was sort of like this: *I knew how to talk with one group of folks, I knew how to talk with the other group of folks, but then when they're all kind of jumbled in there together and they were responding to one another, it was just weird.* I still don't know if I mediated that well or not because it was unexpected. I don't know how to mediate it if I don't anticipate it.

After that, I felt like I was starting to self-censor. I started thinking, "okay, if I post this, these are the possible responses, and then this is what I'll possibly do."

That's when participating on social media started taking up too much of my time. Before that it was just like "oh, here's a link to blah blah blah" or you know x, y, or z, and then I had to start asking myself like "oh my gosh, if I post this, who could possibly comment and what is the array of possible comments and how can I respond back to that to make everyone like just let it go and have a good day, because it's really not anything serious?"

So, that began to take up too much energy, and I kind of backed away from it. I think in these past four weeks I may have posted two status updates.

Self-censoring has made me limit how much I use social media because it's taking up too much of my thinking. If I have to put this much thought into whether I should put something on my Facebook account because of what people might possibly say to each other it just feels really silly and it also just feels like "why in the world do you want to engage in this social media where you can kind of talk about things and say things but you don't want to deal with the fallout of saying them or posting them." I don't know how much energy I want to put into the fallout … but I'd like to maintain some level of civility.

My Facebook page is my page, and if you write something I don't like, I'm going to delete it. Not everything goes on this page, because in some ways I always still feel that it's a reflection of me and the people that I want to have involved in conversation and so it's ultimately my issue if someone's posting and I don't really care about what they have to say because I accepted them and they have access to post. So if I don't like it, I can always change it, … I don't feel like I have to take ownership of people who say things that are bad – they have to live with that – but if it's something that is hurtful, I do feel like it's important for me to either address it in a comment or to delete it, or address it and delete it later. I feel like it would be a bad reflection upon me to not say something if people were being hurtful.

One experience sticks out in my mind on Facebook, because it bothered me. It was about a birthday, and I posted something like "I appreciate that my mother chose to have me," and then it just evolved into this whole debate around pro-life or pro-choice debate, and it just became vicious, because it became about Bible citings and all this stuff, and I was thinking "oh, gosh, no people no!"

I felt a lot of anxiety around it, and kept repeatedly checking the thread. … I hated that feeling, because it wasn't about that at all, it wasn't about trying to one-up somebody or prove my point or make you believe what I believe about it. I really didn't care, that really wasn't part of the comment; it WAS a political statement, but it wasn't one to devolve into who's going to heaven and who's going to hell and who gets to decide that. That really was not the space. So, a lot of the people I used to go to church with aren't on my Facebook any longer.

But, I do try to keep a diverse group of people on there, because I think that even though I haven't posted a lot lately, I think that when those postings were happening it was nice to have dialogue around them. But, how do you get groups of people to talk to each other? Who are my really staunch conservative friends and who are my super liberal friends and is there a way to have a conversation together? The few times that it happened it just pushes a little bit to one side or the other and it just dissolves to something that's not helpful for anybody.

With youth I really try to think about how social media and youth practices in their own culture doesn't get co-opted by my need to make them think something's cool. … I don't want Facebook to be a space where they censor themselves because they think their teachers are going to be looking at what they do. … I think that's probably my only apprehension…. what does this mean to do this kind of social networking with younger people? Because I don't want it to turn into something that isn't theirs or that they don't kind of have ownership over.

Jaime's reflections beg the following questions: What if the starting point to our conversations about social media was that digital participation is complex and varied? How does the personal interact with the professional? What else can we find out about the topic if we started investigating networked scholarship from a non–deterministic point of view?

6

NETWORKS OF TENSION AND CONFLICT

May, 2015.

In an advice column at *Inside Higher Ed*, an online publication focusing on issues of the academy, an anonymous academic asked:

> This year has been full of stories about engaged scholars being targeted for their social media activity. I'm active on Twitter, but as a tenure-track faculty member (I'm just finishing my first year), a scholar of color and a researcher who studies racial inequalities, the cumulative impact of these stories is scaring me and I'm not sure what the takeaway is for me as an individual faculty member. One of my mentors suggested I delete my Twitter account until my tenure decision, but that seems a bit extreme. I want to do research that matters, I want to win tenure at my current university and I can't imagine not being engaged with a broader audience on social media. But right now I just feel deeply unsettled.
>
> *(Confused on the Tenure Track, 2015)*

Although the hope for positive outcomes has led many academics to advocate for the adoption of networked scholarship – and for institutions to encourage scholars to embrace social media in their practice (Mewburn & Thompson, 2013) – scholars' open, digital, and networked activities appear to be rife with tensions, dilemmas, and conundrums. For instance, scholars may often feel uneasy about how their activities on social media might be perceived by students, colleagues, administrators, potential employers, tenure committees, and policymakers.

Writing for the *Chronicle of Higher Education*, Jenkins (2014) notes: "Social media constitutes the classic Catch-22 for academics: We can't ignore it or avoid it, nor do most of us want to, yet it gets us into more trouble than anything else."

Though practitioners like Jaime (chapter 5), Jenkins, and Confused on the Tenure Track highlight the complexities of social media use, proponents for technology-infused approaches to scholarship continue to present an overwhelmingly positive perspective of the potential of technology and networked scholarship. Research on the topic has only recently started to capture the complex tensions that arise when academics engage in new approaches to scholarship. The same critique is often launched against the Educational Technology field and Selwyn (2011, p. 713) charges that an overwhelmingly positive attitude toward technology "limits the validity and credibility of the field as a site of serious academic endeavour." Thus, this chapter seeks to highlight and clarify the tensions, challenges, and compromised realities that occur when social media intersect with academia. Is the anonymous academic above unique? What are the challenges that others are facing? What are online social networks like for the academics that use them? These are some of the questions that networked scholarship must grapple with if it is to become a staple in contemporary higher education.

Illustrative Example: Steven Salaita

Many of the tensions that underlie networked scholarship became visible during the late summer of 2014, with the case of Steven Salaita's "de-hiring" from the University of Illinois at Urbana-Champaign (UIUC).

"Dr. Steven Salaita's rescinded job offer at UIUC" writes Risam (2014), "is the latest incident that has given me pause about the role of Twitter in my academic life." This feeling was shared by many academics at the time.

Salaita, an associate professor of English at Virginia Tech, was offered a tenured position as professor of American Indian Studies at UIUC, subject to a routine approval by the UIUC Board of Trustees. Approved by the Acting Director for the American Indian Studies program, Salaita had accepted the offer, resigned his Virginia Tech position, and was scheduled to teach two courses at UIUC in the fall of 2014 (Jaschik, 2014). Instead, on August 1, 2014, the University of Illinois at Urbana-Champaign effectively rescinded the offer by stating that Salaita's appointment would not go forward to the Board.

By all accounts, Salaita's offer was revoked due to his outspoken tweets criticizing Israel. Throughout July 2014, as Israel launched military operations in Gaza, the Palestinian-descended Salaita registered his opposition publicly – and somewhat hyperbolically – via Twitter. His tweets included statements such as "At this point, if Netanyahu appeared on TV with a necklace made from the teeth of Palestinian children, would anybody be surprised? #Gaza." As *Inside Higher Ed* reported it, "Salaita's tweets have struck some as crossing a line into uncivil behavior" (Jaschik, 2014).

Since Salaita had already resigned his position in Virginia at the time UIUC rescinded his offer, he was without the protection of tenure. He declared the situation an infringement on his academic freedom, and sought reinstatement rather than a financial settlement. University trustees, however, voted down a proposal to reconsider Salaita's employment. The American Association of University Professors (AAUP) Committee A on Academic Freedom and Tenure eventually found that "Professor Salaita's appointment should have entitled him to the due process rights of a tenured faculty member," and UIUC "violated the AAUP/AAC&U 1940 Statement of Principles on Academic Freedom and Tenure" (Reichman, Wallach Scott, & Tiede, 2015). Salaita has since filed a landmark lawsuit against the university and the UIUC Board of Trustees, which was ongoing at the time of writing.

The intersection of the ideal of academic freedom with the realities of networked public speech raises real issues for institutions and individual academics in the contemporary academy. Although scholars are often exhorted to "go online" to promote their research, institutional recognition of networked scholarship often appears to be as much about control, surveillance, or social media policies (Summers, 2014) as about integrating public scholarship into academic criteria for success. The capacity of networked speech acts to reach large and even viral audiences, particularly if in some way controversial, is an uncomfortable reality for institutions in an age of carefully-controlled brand optics and communications.

Salaita's case is a particularly vivid one of the maxim that social media can get scholars fired, but not hired. Published emails obtained through a Freedom of Information Act request indicate that Salaita's provocative public expressions of his political positions resulted in significant objections from university donors (DesGarennes, 2014). This threat of financial consequences, combined with the fact that routine approval of Salaita's position had not yet gone to the university's Board, appear to have led the university to decide that Salaita's public tweets were a liability they could not afford. Whether the ensuing controversy has led them to reconsider that cost-benefit assessment is unclear.

What is clear is that the Salaita case makes visible the limits of academic freedom as protection for scholars' public speech. While Cary Nelson, former president of the AAUP, asserted that the issue was not one of academic freedom since Salaita had not been formally hired, Nelson was criticized as being "disingenuous" (Flaherty, 2014) for his critique. The AAUP itself, as noted above, has found that academic freedom had indeed been violated, and legal scholars including Dorf (2014) have asserted that since Salaita was assured his approval by the UIUC Board of Trustees was a rubber stamp and resigned his Virginia Tech position on that understanding, the University of Illinois should have afforded him academic freedom. Nonetheless, academic freedom no longer covers the majority of academics. While Salaita's lack of tenure protection may have been largely technical in this instance, the fact remains that a vast majority of scholars in contemporary academia do not hold tenured positions. The message to adjuncts and contingent faculty, and to all other early career scholars hoping to secure academic positions, then, is one of "don't rock the boat."

This message is in tension with networked practices in two significant ways.

First, building public identities and robust networks – particularly via Twitter, a hub of engagement for networked academics – demands the cultivation of visibility and attention. Individuals in networks must signal in order to build associations with other individuals. While controversial or provocative signals are not necessary, they do tend to result in amplified attention. Thus, Twitter as a space for public speech rewards a very different type of performance and engagement than the cautious, measured, evidence-based tone valued within conventional scholarship.

Secondly, Twitter speech – at least in Twitter's fledgling years – has tended to be treated as relational, performative, and ephemeral; a casual and informal space for interaction and expression. Yet all digital communications are, as boyd (2011) notes, persistent, replicable, scalable, and searchable, which means tweets with controversial content can be seized upon, screen-captured or retweeted to viral scale, and interpreted out of the context to which they were addressed. Salaita's hyperbolic statements may be more likely to be read as anti-Semitic and uncivil if viewed with the expectations generally applied to written, scholarly assertions rather than to political statements made in a highly performative environment.

However, increasingly, scholars are becoming aware that there are consequences to the ways in which the tenor of Twitter and social media conflicts with that of academia.

Twitter's norms around public speech and speakability have been shifting. In particular, the tactical use of hashtags, which enable widely-distributed individuals to organize and galvanize around issues of common interest, has gained visibility. This "call-out culture" phenomenon, in which tweets deemed problematic are quickly circulated through large-scale networks, has become a widely-reported aspect of Twitter (Ronson, 2015), and has infiltrated scholarly use of Twitter to some extent. Mass Twitter outrage can generate swift offline effects. While call-out culture raises issues of shaming and risk, it has also raised consciousness around the implications of public speech on Twitter.

When combined with the type of institutional consequences experienced by Steven Salaita, however, this rise in tactical uses of Twitter raises the stakes for scholars. While academic Twitter was initially a relatively parochial and collegial circle, it is now thrust into the messy, contested business of being *truly* open to multiple publics at the same time. Scholars who choose to develop networked identities in spite of the risks of scale, virality, and surveillance do report real benefits; networked participation can open doors to visibility and to media and speaking opportunities, particularly for junior, adjunct, and otherwise precariously-positioned scholars whose contributions may receive less notice or validation institutionally (Stewart, 2015a). But between the risks of virality and the increasing "don't rock the boat" messages from institutional corners, early career researchers and others with the most to gain from participation may hesitate to engage.

For those who do engage, the lessons of Steven Salaita are not yet entirely clear. Relational networked spaces like Twitter rely on a blurring of personal and professional voices and contributions, and yet Salaita's case shows vividly that

– particularly with regard to controversial and highly volatile issues – unfiltered personal perspectives can create very significant professional conflicts and consequences. At the same time, Twitter's increasingly heightened identity politics and tactical usage means that, within many social spheres within the network, the signaling of personal alignments and beliefs is a requisite of belonging. People can be called out for their speech, and also for their lack of speech. Thus tensions around social media and networked scholarship are complex, and unlikely to be resolved merely through the lens of academic freedom.

What Are the Tensions? Surveillance, Misaligned Conventions, and Homophily

Scholarly and cultural concerns with technology and social media have arisen that influence adoption of social media and other tools in scholarship. Privacy issues, the "call-out culture" phenomenon described above, and concerns about the encroachment of technology in general have led to hesitancies among some scholars to use social media in professional settings.

Surveillance and Termination

A central concern for many scholars is the degree to which online activities may be surveilled by their institutions and deemed just cause for termination. The Salaita case is not unique; the widely-publicized spring 2015 media storm over Boston University new hire Saida Grundy raised many of the same issues, though Grundy was still – at time of writing – an incoming assistant professor at the university (Brown, 2015).

In 2014, the Kansas Board of Regents instituted a policy governing faculty and staff "improper use of social media" (Colson, 2014) that was somewhat vague and was seen by many as encroaching upon the values of academic freedom. The Kansas policy allowed administrators to discipline or terminate faculty members whose social media activities were seen to be "contrary to the best interest[s] of the university." While social media policies are becoming the norm in academia, and faculty members and administrators need to work together to devise policies that take into account the complex realities that academics and institutions of higher education find themselves in, it is important to recognize the role of culture in conversations pertaining to the use of social media as it relates to academic freedom and freedom of speech. For instance, it is unclear whether Salaita's posts would lead to his firing if he were at a Canadian institution (Raymer, 2015).

Misalignment between the Conventions of Social Media and Academia

To what extent do scholarly systems value and support networked scholarship and its associated practices, such as social media outreach? Is the opportunity cost of such practices too great for scholars to take pioneering risks? Should junior scholars follow the advice given to the anonymous scholar at the beginning of this chapter and delete their social media accounts until after they receive tenure? After all, prior research suggests that "professional seniority [gave them] the confidence to invest time in non-traditional academic production" (Kirkup, 2010, p. 81).

Scholars face an environment which lacks established frameworks of evaluation to judge the legitimacy or quality of their digital activities (Borgman, 2007). The compatibility between social media practices and the current culture of educational systems is thus called into question. This lack of fit was recently documented by Costa (2014), who interviewed 10 active networked scholars to better understand their sense of identity and experiences of online practice. She found that these individuals were "torn between what they perceive[d] to be innovative practices that renew the meaning to their activity and the conventional rules of academia that they [saw] as stifling their novel approaches to scholarly work" (Costa, p. 14). In essence, the conventions of social media practices are not necessarily legible or considered valuable within academia, at least as yet.

As Rogers (2003) explains in his seminal work on the diffusion of innovations, there are many factors which influence the extent to which innovations are adopted on a large scale, including a given innovation's trialability, observability, and complexity. However, the two factors Rogers identifies as most important for the diffusion of any innovation are (1) its relative advantages and (2) its compatibility with the adopting population's beliefs and value systems. The latter is important because of its immediate relevance to the use of technology in scholarship. Ajjan and Hartshorne (2008) found that although 56 percent of faculty studied believed that social networking tools were useful tools for improving student-to-student interaction, 74 percent did not plan on using them in their instruction. Similar findings applied to blogging, social bookmarking, and wikis. The *Chronicle of Higher Education* reported similar findings: of 4,600 faculty surveyed from 50 US colleges and universities in 2009, only 16 percent were using collaborative editing software (e.g., wikis) and only 13 percent used blogs in their teaching (Coddington, 2010). Though, as we have seen, these numbers have increased since 2008 and 2009, the discrepancy between beliefs and actual utilization identified by Ajjan and Hartshorne appears to persist.

This discrepancy is impacted heavily by the incompatibility between professors' practices and participatory technologies. In other words, the way that higher education coursework is generally constructed, organized, and delivered is structurally different from how social media may construct relationships between individuals and content/faculty, with many academics (and students) believing that it is inappropriate for scholars to have accounts on social media sites (Malesky & Peters, 2012). Thus, as the "conventions of a rather conservative academic world," as Costa puts it, are not aligned with the conventions of the participatory web, adoption suffers.

To this end – and as it concerns scholarly activity – researchers have argued that departmental and institutional policies for promotion and tenure may need to be revised to recognize and reward a broader set of scholarly practices than traditionally rewarded (Greenhow & Gleason, 2014). Such calls often align with the rise of the *alternative metrics* (altmetrics) movement which calls for the development of metrics other than citation counts and journal impact factors to evaluate the impact of scholarly practice outside of academia (Priem & Hemminger, 2010; Priem et al., 2010).

Homophily and Filtering

While social media participation might offer opportunities for scholars to connect with diverse audiences, scholars need to remain vigilant about technology's potential to reinforce existing power structures and norms. The tendency to connect with similar or like-minded individuals online as offline, which Thelwall (2009) calls homophily, means that social media may not foster diverse spaces for knowledge exchange and negotiation but lead instead to "echo chambers." In this view of networked practices, engaged individuals are more inclined to share knowledge and perspectives with individuals with similar or aligned worldviews.

At the same time, social media algorithms may also shape the information that scholars access online. Algorithms that are intended to support personalization may blind users to diversity and encourage uniformity. Pariser (2011) describes this phenomenon as the "filter bubble" and presents a convincing array of examples in which Internet tools have limited users' exposure to diverse information because web algorithms are designed to retrieve information that they deem relevant to the user. In the case of scholars, relevance might refer to search engines filtering research from the same or similar discipline or social media recommending familiar connections (e.g., recommendations on LinkedIn to connect with people one has exchanged emails with) or connections that share similar characteristics (e.g., recommendations on Twitter to connect with people who share connections).

Given the potential scholarly benefits of connecting with individuals who might not share the same perspectives or social networks with us, algorithmic filtering may pose a wide array of obstacles to scholars. For instance, even though I appreciate connecting with individuals in my own discipline of learning technologies, I could also learn a lot from sociologists and cognitive scientists who study technology, but filtering algorithms may limit my exposure to them. Matters become more complex because most, if not all, of the algorithms that are used to retrieve relevant information or make recommendations for web users are "black box" algorithms, meaning that the user has no insight into how his/her input (e.g., keyword) generates the outputs (e.g., search results) that s/he is presented with. For instance, Google Scholar does not make visible or public the processes by which it generates the results that it does. Technologies with black box algorithms can also be found within institutions. Summon, for example, is a one-stop gateway to search institutional library resources – its relevance ranking algorithm operates as a black box.

What are the Tensions? The Lived Experiences of Three Faculty Members

The majority of the research examining scholars' use of social media focuses upon what scholars do online, the impact of their actions, and how they perceive their networked/digital practices. There's much less research examining *how they experience* their online activities. In Veletsianos and Kimmons (2013) we explored how scholars experience their use of social networking sites, and a lot of what we discovered centred on the tensions and conundrums of this practice.

Our goal was to understand the day-to-day reality of social media use. We interviewed three academics who, at the time of our interviews, worked at a large research-intensive university. I'll refer to these individuals with the pseudonyms Barry, Cassandra, and Julie. Barry was a tenured associate professor who used Facebook occasionally and claimed to have a "neutral to negative outlook" toward it. Cassandra was a former elementary school teacher and a relatively new assistant professor who wished to use Facebook as a professional tool. Julie was a fairly new assistant professor and used Facebook to connect with her family members, students, and colleagues.

One conundrum that Barry, Cassandra, and Julie reported centred on the **time demands and commitments of the scholarly profession**. Many faculty members acutely feel the time commitment of their careers. Ziker and colleagues (2014) studied faculty work days at Boise State University and found that, on average, the 30 faculty members that participated in their study worked 61 hours per week. These results are not unsurprising, and as a consequence, scholars may be aware how easily their work can encroach upon their home lives. In our interviews we found that Barry, Cassandra, and Julie were critical of technological tools that are inefficient, do not improve work activities, or make work activities more ubiquitous. Social networking sites (SNS) were seen as problematic, because they often collapse personal and professional activities, and are commonly used outside of the office. In Barry's words:

> online access, email, and social networking add to the complexity of those who struggle with the home-work balance. … My hunch is that [SNS use] would only add to the kind of struggles I'm [concerned] about in terms of time on computer and time away from personal contact.

For such faculty, social media use can be seen as detracting from real-life interaction and experiences, and as providing little more than entertainment value. Barry continued: "there are a few people I would follow on Twitter that I'd get a kick out of what they say. But for me, the trade-off of that one interesting thing … is not really worth it." From Barry's perspective, social media usage would be inefficient for pursuing professional goals.

On the other hand, Julie viewed social media as a potentially efficient means of communicating with students and colleagues. Rather than sending out a question to a mailing list, for instance, faculty can post questions on social media, which they might perceive as less intrusive than sending a bulk email. Social media also allows for instant feedback. Likewise, it enables faculty to connect with students in a manner that is more personal and familiar. Depending upon the professor's goals, this may or may not make sense in practice. Social media also allow for connections with peers as well as students. According to Julie, "my position [as a professor] is building a community of teachers that I talk to … where you can share, and so it makes total sense [to share through social media]." So, if developing a community is the faculty member's goal, then it seems that some view social media use to be an efficient method for achieving this goal. Julie's perspectives parallel the ways that Anna (chapter 3) described her social media activities and views.

Nonetheless, Barry, Cassandra, and Julie were concerned about constraints upon their time and did not willingly seek out new technologies that might make their lives more cluttered or less efficient. With regard to social media, Cassandra says "it definitely takes away time," but her real question was whether or not the time spent with social media would be used in a valuable way to achieve a desired goal. "At the end of the day," Cassandra said, "it's become more about time and time management … I keep thinking I should be writing or looking at data, and I'm doing this!"

A second conundrum that Barry, Cassandra, and Julie reported to us focused on the **necessity of intentionally establishing and maintaining professional and personal boundaries** when sharing information on social media about themselves. On the one hand, Barry explained: "I think that it's okay for students to not know everything about their professor." Cassandra expressed similar feelings. From this perspective, these professors are careful in determining what to share and whom to share it with. On the other hand though, Julie said: "[T]here's nothing in my personal life that I wouldn't feel comfortable with my students knowing."

Nonetheless, all three are conscious of boundaries, recognize the necessity of having clearly established boundaries, and carefully consider whether or not to connect with students and other faculty/staff. They recognize that the people they connect with online will influence their social media experiences and the traces they themselves leave online. For that reason, some preferred to keep private things private and limit their Facebook friends list. Even when these three faculty members openly connected with others on social media, they were careful to make boundaries clear both for themselves and those they connected with. Julie explained that though she connects with her students, she uses the SNS to teach them about necessary professional boundaries. Though she may feel that her own boundaries "are so clear that there's less need to pronounce them," her students nonetheless need guidance in establishing boundaries, especially if they are at a stage in life that includes certain behaviours like dating or "partying," that might be potentially problematic for professional growth (e.g., securing a job). As Julie explained, "I don't have anything in my life where if somebody posted something of me it would be a problem. I'm also not looking for a job."

Failure to consciously establish boundaries was perceived by these faculty members as leading to problems. Cassandra for example, had failed to establish clear boundaries around how and with whom she would interact at the outset of her social media use, and as a result, it required an inordinate amount of time for her to continue to successfully function within the environment. Her experience of social media had become something she hadn't anticipated or wanted. Such a lack of clearly established boundaries can make navigation of online social networks difficult for faculty members, such that their use of the tool becomes stressful.

Barry, Cassandra, and Julie also indicated that learning to successfully establish boundaries, though difficult at first, does improve with time. Whereas participants reported that they initially needed to create rules with regard to whom to accept as a friend and whom to reject, the rules tended to become second nature. This suggests that Barry, Cassandra, and Julie gradually learned the literacies necessary to navigate social media, such that they no longer had to focus on the rules of boundary setting and could function effectively without analyzing every potential connection in relation to boundaries.

Nonetheless, faculty are wise to consider intentionally establishing and maintaining professional and personal boundaries. Three popular ways that I have observed that scholars use to manage personal–professional boundaries are: having multiple profiles on social media (e.g., one professional, one personal); using some social media (e.g., Facebook) for personal purposes and others (e.g., Twitter) for professional purposes; and curtailing their participation on social media to ensure that all messages are appropriate for personal and professional audiences.

This third way of managing personal–professional boundaries on social media was one we uncovered in our research with Barry, Cassandra, and Julie, where we discovered that scholars **structured their online participation in particular ways so as to shape the ways that others saw them**. As early as 2008, Tufekci described how some activities that play a role in career advancement (e.g., social grooming, presentation of the self) are becoming more and more prevalent in online spaces. Barry, Cassandra, and Julie all saw their activity within social media as an extension of their professional and personal identities and believed that others would draw conclusions about who they were based upon their participation and connections. Even though faculty believe that their social media use reflects them as a person and a professional, they may not feel that they are in complete control of their social media image, and may thus curtail participation overall so as to be sure to present an acceptable self to the world.

A complicating factor is that, although individuals control what they share (or do not share) online, they do not always know how others will view their activities. Barry wondered how others would see him if he decided to share personal photographs, and whether others would be able to connect with him on a personal level if he chose not to share. As he explained: "When I had no pictures up there and like no pictures of my wife up there, people wondered why." Thus, both action *and* inaction were seen as potential reflections of the self.

Though faculty members saw their own actions and inactions as reflecting upon their identities, they also noted how the actions and inactions of their networks can impact presence and identities. An innocuous posting by a professor can quickly turn into something problematic if reacted to or amplified by others. If faculty members fail to anticipate how people within their networks will interact with others through them, they may feel accountable for any uncivil or inappropriate interactions between their connections. Public threaded communications on a scholar's own page or feed can be viewed as a reflection upon the scholar himself or herself, prompting action from some to prevent or correct problems. Constant oversight and management, however, is difficult to maintain and can lead to stress and discomfort. As a result, faculty members may seek a certain level of predictability in their connections as a preventive measure against having to constantly weed out problematic interactions. As Cassandra noted,

> There have been some people that I went to graduate school with recently that are not very stable. ... When they try to add me, I decline/ignore, because ... I try to think about who you were in class with me and with other people and there's no way I want that garbage. I don't want to deal with it.

This suggests that faculty members believe that the people they connect with have a measure of power in determining how others view them and, therefore, are accepted only if they can be trusted to act "with a certain level of civility" and predictability.

To summarize, diverse groups of people who are connected with scholars collectively and continuously produce and re-create scholars' online identity. Thus scholars may tend to feel that they must manage their social media spaces, because those spaces reflect upon them as people and professionals.

Conclusion

In the social media experiences of faculty members, conundrums and tensions appear between personal connections and professional responsibilities and image. Scholars appear to be highly aware of their actions and the expectations placed upon them in relationship to their professional and personal commitments, but may find themselves in the spotlight nonetheless. The tensions that may arise from the use of technologies that collapse personal and professional contexts and audiences are significant. Combined with scale or size of account, context collapse between heretofore separate audiences is a key risk area for unwanted attention, especially when messages intended for an imagined professional or personal audience end up going viral or being exposed to unanticipated audiences. While research suggests that faculty members may actively attempt to manage the ways they present themselves, this research also shows that the activities of others may impact how faculty members are perceived.

While many challenges arise because of context collapse, they also stem from the fact that technology is not neutral (Hall, 2011; Lane, 2009; Whitworth & Benson, 2010). As technologies designed for non-scholarly purposes are appropriated into educational settings, their embedded values and norms may be in conflict with the values and norms of higher education cultures or with the ways that scholars would like to use them. Since social media are negotiated spaces with embedded values, we should recognize that practices developing in conjunction with emergent technologies will be influenced by the embedded values (often hidden in black box algorithms) of those technologies and that not all of these influences may be positive. For example, though Google search gives scholars quick access to a wide array of resources, the presentation of such resources may be biased by researchers' previous searches or by dominant cultural trends or norms, thereby hiding conflicting evidence. Additionally, though Twitter allows researchers to follow one another and discuss topics of interest, assumptions and conclusions may go unchallenged if participants are only followed by those who have similar educational training and beliefs.

Scholars can counteract some of the tensions they face on social media by creating rules on whom to connect with, among other strategies. But scholars' participation in online social networks could also be supported by platforms providing users with audience controls (e.g., Google Plus allows individuals to share information with individuals placed in distinct groups called *circles*) or with opportunities to switch easily between activity streams (e.g., from professional to personal streams). Such affordances would offer academics increased agency in interacting with diverse audiences. When platforms and technology companies demand or prescribe particular modes of participation (e.g., requiring users to use their real names), they contribute to tensions and thus to social media underuse or rejection.

7

NICHOLAS: A VISITOR

"Nicholas" is a composite character that I created to illustrate the activities and characteristics of "visitor" behaviour on social media. Nicholas could be a mid-career faculty member in a North American or European institution holding a research-intensive or teaching-intensive position in any number of disciplines. It's also possible that Nicholas could be an early-career faculty member – visitors and residents are differentiated by outlook and usage rather than by age, profession, social location or technical skill level. The description of Nicholas that follows draws from a number of studies conducted on the topic.

While the research on digital scholarly practices often focuses on heavy users, such as Anna (chapter 3), the majority of scholars do not appear to adopt social media in extensive, or even imaginative, ways. Thus, Nicholas serves as an example of how the majority of scholars are currently using social media in their life. White and LeCornu (2011) argue that while visitors tend to see digital environments in tool-oriented or instrumental terms, residents operate from a relational sense of place and presence with others. From resident perspectives, the value of a digital environment is "assessed in terms of relationships as well as knowledge" (White & LeCornu, 2011, IV.2 Residents section, ¶ 2), with identity, profiles and belonging all foregrounded. However, "even Twitter and blogs can be approached in the less-visible visitor mode when people use them to consume rather than produce Internet content" (Connaway, Lanclos, & Hood, 2013, Mode and Mode Combinations section, ¶ 5). Individuals vary in their use of tools and ways they engage with these technologies, so there's no standard with regard to how "visitors" to networked scholarship behave.

The description that follows is intended to provide a snapshot of just one individual in order to problematize the concept of networked scholarship and recognize that scholars' digital participation online varies widely between people.

The visitors-residents continuum suggests that individuals may be visitors in some contexts and residents in others.

Nicholas' use of social media in his personal and professional life can be described as goal-oriented, and compartmentalized. Unlike Anna, social media are neither infused in all aspects of Nicholas' life nor are they integrated across professional and personal contexts. To illustrate Nicholas' digital and networked participation, I created a Visitors-Residents map for him as shown in Figure 7.1.

Nicholas tends to use a variety of social software, the most prominent of which are Facebook, Twitter, LinkedIn, Skype, Google Plus, Google Scholar, and his institutional email. If he were interviewed he would likely have said that he reads traditional media, like the *New York Times* or the *Guardian*. He reads these mostly online, but may do so offline as well. Overall, he enjoys reading what his colleagues may post on social media and finds some of their posts amusing and informative, but in conversation he would quickly note he won't "go looking for funny animals or memes online" or seek to cultivate and nurture a thriving digital presence. In fact, like many scholars, even ones that are heavy users, Nicholas is averse to the idea of branding and promoting himself online. Further he believes that such innocuous terms as *digital identity management* are ways to make branding more palatable to greater numbers of scholars who may resist such self-promotion.

Asked how he found out about various social media such as LinkedIn and Twitter, Nicholas tries to recall those particular times, but his answers often boil down to him having heard of the tools from colleagues or from mass media. It's

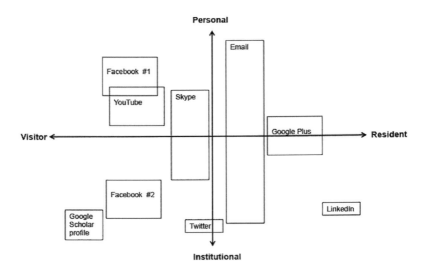

FIGURE 7.1 Visitors-Residents Map for "Nicholas"

very rare for him to experiment with new technologies before others and even when he tries new technologies on the recommendation of others, he often questions the point of the technology. This is particularly true of Twitter. He might ask questions like the following: "What's the point of writing updates that are only 140-characters long? What do I care about what other people have for breakfast? How is Twitter helpful to my life and career?"

Nicholas also has trouble verbalizing the positive impact that some of these tools have on him. For instance, he might say

> I use LinkedIn professionally. … I mean, I accept friend requests, I send requests for connecting with others, I read messages that are posted in various professional groups I belong, but I'm not sure if the networking aspect of these technologies is of much help. … I am able to efficiently find out about conferences or publication opportunities … but to be honest I'm not really sure who my connections are on the platform. … I guess there are ways that I could do better. For example if I travel somewhere I could look up my colleagues in the area. … I just haven't done that.

Returning to the map, Nicholas uses three technologies in resident status: email, Google Plus, and LinkedIn. Nicholas sees his email as closely tied to his professional identity even though he uses it to communicate with non-professional contacts, too. He keeps a profile on Google Plus, courtesy of Google's persistent encouragement, but has not posted any updates nor has he changed the default profile picture provided. His use of Google Plus is limited to Hangouts, a videoconferencing tool integrated with Google Plus that allows him to call colleagues and friends. Finally, Nicholas can be categorized as a "resident" on LinkedIn because he maintains a profile on that site, manages his connections, and updates his profile semi-frequently. Nicholas uses LinkedIn for strictly professional purposes and keeps it separate from aspects of identity that are known to friends and family (e.g., his political and religious beliefs, hobbies).

The rest of the tools that Nicholas uses serve specific goals and are used with relative caution.

While Nicholas keeps a Twitter profile he uses it sporadically. He might not post updates for weeks at a time, but he often uses it more heavily when at a conference. When at a conference, he is most likely to browse to the conference hashtag, browse the stream, and retweet posts by others. His use of Twitter centres on professional purposes and, overall, he consumes many more tweets than he produces.

Nicholas maintains two Facebook accounts: Facebook #1 is a personal account that he makes available to face-to-face friends and family, while Facebook #2 is a professional account which he uses to connect with colleagues and students. Nicholas has established rules to decide who to connect with and how. For instance, (a) university administrators are only allowed in Facebook #2, and (b) at the beginning of every course, current students who are connected with him on Facebook #1 are sent messages to be unfriended and are asked to reconnect with him at the conclusion of the course. Such rules are extensive, but serve to demarcate professional and personal activities. Importantly, some colleagues are close enough friends to be on Facebook #1. Nonetheless, Nicholas' activity on both his personal and professional Facebook accounts is sporadic and limited. Like Twitter, he visits Facebook relatively infrequently.

Nicholas uses Skype to have meetings with friends and colleagues and this tool is used more frequently than Google Plus. Nicholas shares his Skype username with individuals he intends to have conversations with at the time that this is needed, and it is not shared publicly. For example, his Skype username is not posted on his institutional website or email signature

To consume videos, largely for personal purposes, Nicholas uses YouTube. He may at times show videos in his courses, but does not upload videos to the platform. He does not follow other users on the platform.

As a scholar who tends to approach social networks from a visitor's perspective, Nicholas represents a broad set of commonly-encountered assumptions about social media. These assumptions extend from mechanical understandings of tools, and tend to exclude the social or relational elements of networks.

8

NETWORKS OF INEQUITY

It is imperative to recognize that networked scholarship is neither a panacea, nor a solution without its own shortcomings. In this chapter, I explore how (a) productive participation in networks requires an understanding of the social and digital literacies and skills essential for effective engagement with such networks, and yet (b) social stratification and exclusion in online environments and networks is reinforced. Inequity permeates online networks in a similar way that it permeates other organizational structures. Put differently, even though social media may enable participation by anyone, anywhere, at any time, a number of variables moderate and mediate that participation. Thus, while Friedman (2005) argued that digital technologies might "flatten" the world to create a more even playing field, and Bonk (2009) asserted that digital technologies could democratize education, as social media platforms mature their democratizing potential and inclusive nature is increasingly called into question.

#YesAllWomen

People often encounter the darker side of humanity on social media. Technology-based practices and experiences are mediated by economic, political, and social factors, and reflect the cultures that we live in. Thus the harassment, threats, abuse, misogyny, and attempts at silencing that are part of those broader cultures are also present online and in social networks. The harrowing experiences that sometimes women have online are increasingly visible in social media, although women have been the subjects of online harassment for many years (Lee, 1997). Watters (2014) argues that the prevalence of harassment and threats against women online – particularly prominent women who dare to voice opinions – is an educational technology issue. Watters asserts that online misogyny impacts technology use in higher education because of the expectations that we all are supposed to interact online – for professional, personal, and academic purposes … because we must address the culture of misogyny that permeates so much of the technology industry, particularly as we bring more and more of [it] … into education.

Female scholars and students are encouraged to "go online" because of the opportunities available in online spaces, yet the medium's potential for harm and abuse needs to be factored into any expectations placed on social media uptake in higher education.

At the same time, social media can not only be a site of vitriol against women, but a space for women and allies to speak back against harassment and abuse.

In late May 2014, the hashtag #YesAllWomen trended globally on English-speaking Twitter. Like all hashtags, #YesAllWomen served to collate the contributions of networked strangers around a topic of shared interest – in the case of #YesAllWomen, the hashtag assembled and illustrated the widespread experience of sexism, misogyny, and harrassment among girls and women.

While not the first hashtag employed to raise awareness of the pervasiveness and normativity of sexism, #YesAllWomen achieved a level of virality that previous efforts had not. This was, in part, likely due to widespread horror at the Isla Vista, California, murder spree on May 23, 2014, and the YouTube video and manifesto released by the killer, Elliot Rodger. In the video, Rodger – a 22-year-old, self-proclaimed virgin, sitting behind the wheel of his BMW – asserted that the murders were retribution for his having been ignored by women. When these statements became public in the hours after the killings, Rodger's blatant sense of entitlement to women as sexual objects chilled many, generating condemnation of the Men's Rights Activist websites in which Rodger had made clear he was active.

Like many Internet critiques of sexist practices, however, this groundswell led to deployment of counternarratives – in this case, it led to the deployment of the #NotAllMen hashtag. Tactically, #NotAllMen derails and deflects from discussions of sexism by asserting that "not all individual men are like that," thus re-centring focus on the hurt feelings of men rather than on the harm experienced by women. #NotAllMen came out in full force after the Isla Vista killer's manifesto was released.

Rebecca Solnit (2014) noted that the #NotAllMen outpouring was an effort to shift "the conversation from actual corpses and victims as well as perpetrators to protecting the comfort level of bystander males" (section #YesAllWomen, ¶ 3). Instead of being silenced, however, Twitter took #NotAllMen's game and turned it on itself. Twitter users called for the use of #YesAllWomen to detail women's experiences with the misogyny and entitlement heard in Rodger's rants. The hashtag spread quickly across social media platforms, and was used to share stories of inequality, harassment, violence, and everyday, casual sexism. Some well-known public figures lent their voices to #YesAllWomen, which helped to amplify the hashtag to trending status. Over a period of a few days at the end of May 2014, the hashtag gathered more than 1.2 million tweets (YesAllWomen, 2015).

The majority of contributors, however, were simply regular people. Both male and female voices tweeted to the #YesAllWomen hashtag, and it also made appearances on Facebook and other social networking sites that enable hashtag collation. However, the reasons it remained primarily a Twitter phenomenon may not be limited to the fact that it – like all hashtags – originated on Twitter.

Rather, many women commented anecdotally that the act of contributing publicly to #YesAllWomen or even acknowledging #YesAllWomen was more comfortable for them on Twitter than on Facebook, due to the significant collapse of personal and professional audiences that's common in Facebook. Women who had shared deeply personal #YesAllWomen tweets expressed ambivalence or concern about posting the same content on Facebook, or even acknowledging the hashtag. As one female scholar noted in a closed Facebook discussion thread (quoted with permission)

> Facebook's reciprocality means I sometimes end up in the circles of people who aren't so much ties of choice as of circumstances. So I feel constrained by exactly the kind of misogyny the hashtag speaks against – I have "friends" and friends of friends who would take up #YesAllWomen as an invitation to #NotAllMen all over my feed, and I'm not up for that exposure and exhaustion. I'll keep it on Twitter where at least I don't have to knowingly face my trolls at the grocery store.

In the long run, #YesAllWomen didn't solve the issue of misogyny online, nor even necessarily mitigate it – but it did raise awareness among a huge swath of social media users. It brought attention to the issue and, perhaps more importantly, made many users aware of tactical ways to band together to push back against degradation and misogyny in the public sphere. As Solnit (2014) noted, that awareness and the language to talk about it made a difference:

> The realms of gender shifted a little. They shifted not because of the massacre, but because millions came together in a vast conversational network to share experiences, revisit meanings and definitions, and arrive at new understandings.
>
> *(Crimes Small and Large section, ¶ 5)*

None of this is to suggest that Twitter's capacity to allow people from disparate networks to gather and galvanize over topics of shared interest is inherently emancipatory. While the ways in which Twitter operates not only technically but socially and interpersonally did shape the success of #YesAllWomen, they also shaped and enabled the earlier rise and ongoing persistence of #NotAllMen. And Twitter, both as a platform and as a company, has been notoriously reluctant to address the ways in which its affordances do sometimes enable trolling and harassment. CEO Dick Costolo acknowledged in February 2015, in a series of leaked memos, that "we [Twitter] suck at dealing with abuse" (Tiku & Newton, 2015).

Only time will tell whether his stated commitment to changing that ends up aligning more with #NotAllMen or with #YesAllWomen.

On Literacies, Power, and Inequity

As already explored, online social networks are often presented as sites of benefit for scholars, or as opportunities to improve scholarly effectiveness and efficiency. Research supports the notion of benefits: Kirkup (2010) suggests academic blogging offers an opportunity for scholars to develop their voices publicly. Gruzd, Wellman, and Takhteyev (2011) found that social media platforms help scholars build relationships in their areas of research, while Hurt and Yin (2006) assert that participatory scholarship allows pre-tenured scholars to network with more senior and higher status faculty, increasing junior scholars' visibility and reputations. Stewart's (2015a) work builds on this to suggest that networked scholarship is a channel by which scholars can develop new forms of public, academic influence.

To benefit from networks, however, scholars not only need to understand the participatory nature of the web, they also need to develop the social and digital literacies and skills essential for effective engagement with such networks (cf. Coiro et al., 2008). Unequal access to technology and/or lack of digital literacies is referred to as the participation gap (Jenkins et al., 2006). In the context of networked scholarship, the participation gap refers to those scholars who participate in networked spaces and are able to take advantage of digital literacies to advance their learning, teaching, research, and career vis-a-vis those who have had no exposure to participatory cultures or who do not have the essential literacies to engage in such activities online. Rheingold (2010) is convinced that individuals need literacies affording them to decode and encode digital information, and these literacies relate to attention, participation, collaboration, network awareness, and critical consumption. Additional literacies related to learning new pedagogical approaches, bringing research to the attention of broad audiences, organizing colleagues to tackle professional issues, and grappling with the implications of online identity are all central to effective participation in academic networks. Without access to these literacies, scholars may not be able to take advantage of networked online spaces.

Dealing with knowledge abundance is another key literacy for participation in online networks, and in contemporary scholarship more broadly. Authors argue that the volume of information online has skyrocketed (Aro & Olkinuora, 2007) and that the information age has produced a data "deluge" (Baker, 2008) or "explosion" (Delen & Al-Hawamdeh, 2009). While information overload is hardly a new concept, scholars' experiences of it are amplified by the increasing availability of scholarly publications online, the extensive data trails left behind by social media participation, and the ease with which scholars can access resources from a diverse range of sources and media, from books to newspapers to YouTube.

These new manifestations of abundance combine to create information management challenges for scholars, involving (a) keeping up-to-date with newly published information, (b) filtering information, (c) rapidly differentiating between helpful and irrelevant information, and (d) saving helpful information for future retrieval. Though networked practices afford scholarly opportunities such as efficient information sharing, such efficiencies may create bottlenecks for other aspects of scholarly endeavor, including differentiating between important and peripheral information. To overcome this challenge, scholars need to develop skills, devise methods, and utilize technologies to efficiently collect, categorize, and retrieve digital information pertinent to their work and their digital participation.

One example of a viable technological solution to information management challenges is RSS readers and aggregators. RSS readers are applications that, with the click of a subscribe button, allow users to sign up to receive notices of new content from other scholars and writers they find interesting. These applications monitor feeds and download new posts as they become available. Users of RSS feeds no longer need to visit sites in search of content, but can efficiently retrieve information relevant to their professional interests via blogs, Twitter feeds, journal feeds, and other sources of continuously updated information (Figure 8.1). However, users still need to filter and archive the information that comes in through RSS. As a result, scholars may find that while technological tools may be very effective for dealing with information management challenges, solutions often engender new challenges.

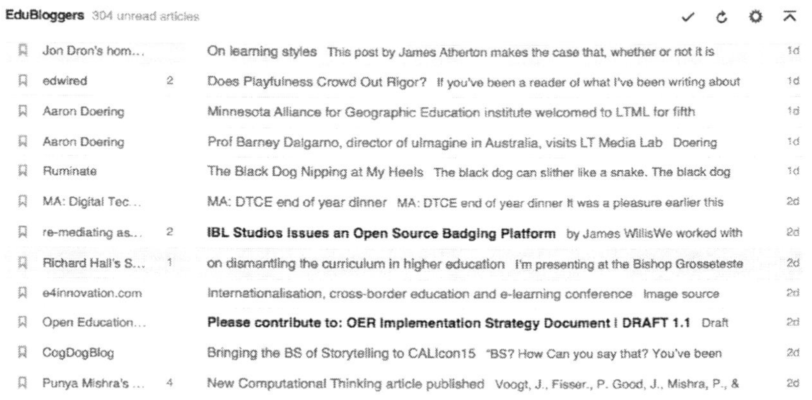

FIGURE 8.1 Screenshot of RSS feeds

Moreover, merely developing digital literacies, effectively using technologies, and participating in online scholarly communities does not mean that scholars will necessarily become equal participants in online spaces. While digital literacies, and an understanding of social technologies, may enable scholars to effectively participate online, it does not necessarily follow that participation will be without perils or inequities. As illustrated by the misogyny that sparked #YesAllWomen, networks often reflect and reinforce societal biases. And emerging research from a variety of fields is supporting this argument. Sajuria et al. (2015) for example, show that traditional structures and behaviours occurring offline are reproduced on social media, thus, once again, calling into question deterministic perspectives on technology. Social stratification and exclusion in online environments and networks can preclude particular voices from being heard in the same ways that others might be. "The inconvenient truth about social media" writes Hermida (2015, p. 1) "is that most tweets, photos, and videos simply wither in the perpetual onslaught of information." Such disparities are referred to by the term *digital divide* – an interwoven and multifaceted issue that is ultimately about equity.

Questions of equity and access go far beyond networked scholarship. Servon (2002, p. 12) writes, "A troubling cycle has begun to take shape, in which the lack of access to information technology and its requisite skills contributes both to an inability to compete in the mainstream economy and an inability to participate in civil society." Whereas social media potentially allow democratic participation, enabling individuals to publish their thoughts widely without institutionalized gatekeepers, citizens' access to technology may be deeply constrained by economic and geographic circumstances. Identity factors may also limit the way or extent to which particular voices are heard on social media, excluding and privileging differing users due to factors outside those individuals' realms of control or influence. Therefore, social media can be seen as another medium through which societal inequalities and the "digital divide" are perpetuated. Solomon, Allen, and Resta (2003) perhaps sum it up best when they state that "race, gender, cultural heritage, linguistic ability, physical ability, and income still define who has access and the quality of that access."

Inequalities on social media do not occur along isolated axes, but are intersectional (Crenshaw, 1989), shaped by multiple dimensions of systemic and structural inequality. Thus the experiences of women of colour, for instance, or women with disabilities, may be very different from those of women who are culturally dominant in the context in which they engage. Cottom (2015a) examines the intersectional operations of online abuse in her paper "'Who Do You Think You Are?': When Marginality Meets Academic Microcelebrity." Cottom is an early-career scholar – a PhD candidate at the time her paper was published – who fits the profile of a networked public intellectual, and whose writing has appeared in numerous media outlets including the *Chronicle of Higher Education* and the *New York Times*. She notes that how her words and identity are received varies according to audience and platform, but also differs from the dominant narrative of sexualized harassment that #YesAllWomen embodied.

> I am not just a woman but also a black woman performing a particular type of expertise for large, multiple publics. As such, my experience of negative comments differs from the dominant gendered narrative of online abuse. For example, I have never received a single rape threat. ... At my blog, engagement with multiple publics has introduced a greater number of informed, respectful readers. Many email me or send me comments about how they appreciate reading a perspective so different from their own ... [But] whereas white women tend to report a significant number of rape threats when they write publicly, the overwhelming threat issued in my comment section and inbox are threats to my academic credibility. I have received 11 death threats, 19 threats of what could be considered general bodily harm, and exactly zero rape threats in three years of writing to over a million readers.
>
> *(Cottom, ¶ 2)*

Cottom's experiences point out vividly the ways in which gender and race mediate individuals' experiences of online participation, as well as the ways in which they intersect with institutional status to mediate experiences of scholarly participation online. Further, Cottom (2015b) analyzes the ways in which these inequalities are becoming embedded within the algorithmic structures of networked platforms, suggesting that targeted Facebook ads based on people's searches and social contacts may affect life chances. She asserts, "a 'personalized' platform can never be democratizing when the platform operates in a society defined by inequalities" (Cottom, 2015b, ¶ 8).

Thus, while social networking platforms offer academics freedom to share and collaborate, they are also spaces where the freedom to abuse, exploit, and limit is endemic. We should be careful not to indulge in idealized notions of participation, sharing, and openness that may be misguided or naive. This becomes particularly important when advocating that non–English-speaking scholars, marginalized scholars, scholars in precarious positions, neurodiverse scholars, or scholars with visual impairments engage in networked scholarship. As Chander and Sunder (2004, p. 1332) argue when discussing what they term *the romance of the public domain*, "[c]ontemporary scholarship extolling the public domain presumes a landscape where each person can reap the riches found in the commons [equally] ... [b]ut, in practice, differing circumstances – including knowledge, wealth, power, and ability – render some better able than others to exploit a commons." Thus, researchers and practitioners alike need to consider who profits from, and who can efficiently and practically use, their collaborative or shared work. As a simple illustration of this issue, while some advocate that scholars should publish in open access journals or that they should use social media in their professional practice, we must recognize that if we engage professionally with these practices ourselves, our advocacy comes from a position of power and we might be better positioned to benefit from these practices than others whose individual circumstances prevent them from fully adopting them.

In short, these arguments call into question whether social media truly are the equalizing forces they are sometimes portrayed to be.

Power by the Numbers

Inequities present themselves online in many different ways. They are visible experientially as I have shown above, but they are also visible statistically. Beyond reinforcing societal power differentials around race, class, gender, and other identity markers, social media platforms enact their own power differentials around who is "able to command attention, influence others' attention, and otherwise traffic in information" (boyd, 2009).

The structural positions that individuals cultivate and inhabit within given networks can be wide-ranging. In Veletsianos and Kimmons (2015), we gathered data pertaining to 469 education scholars' participation on Twitter. Of these individuals, 232 were graduate students and 237 were professors. For each user we captured a variety of data summarizing their Twitter participation, including the number of followers that each person had and the number of tweets each person had posted. We were curious to see whether we could identify differences in participation. We also wanted to understand what factors impacted Twitter participation and what participation looked like for this group of scholars. Based on our qualitative work, we expected to see differences in participation patterns, and hoped that a larger data set would provide more convincing evidence for the types of inequities we observed qualitatively.

Our results showed that participation patterns differ significantly. Scholars' popularity (average number of followers as a percentage of all followers in the sample) and activity (number of tweets) is summarized in Table 8.1. The table provides an overview by percentile groups and can be read as follows: the first row shows that, on average, the top 1 percent of scholars have more than 15,000 followers each on average and as a group command 21 percent of all followers in the sample, while they contribute only 7 percent of the total number of tweets in the sample. In contrast, the top 5 percent of scholars each has more than 4,000 followers on average and as a group command 43 percent of all followers in the sample, while they contribute 29 percent of the total number of tweets in the sample.

Comparing the top 50 percent with the bottom 50 percent of scholars (in terms of popularity) suggests a somewhat meritocratic view of scholarly following, wherein popularity is roughly equivalent to activity: contributing 90 percent of total tweets is associated with 91 percent of all followers, and contributing 10 percent of total tweets is associated with 9 percent of all followers.

TABLE 8.1 Scholars' Popularity and Activity on Twitter

Percentile Group	Popularity (average # of followers)	Popularity (% of followers)	Activity (# of tweets)
top 1%	15,059	21%	7%
top 5%	4,385	43%	29%
top 10%	1,389	57%	45%
top 50%	140	91%	90%
bottom 50%	22	9%	10%
bottom 99%	164	79%	93%

However, this meritocratic view breaks down as we consider the upper echelons of scholars, wherein the top 5 percent garner 43 percent of all followers, while only providing 29 percent of all tweets, and the top 1 percent garner 21 percent of all followers, while providing only 7 percent of all tweets. These differences become starker, when we consider that the top 1 percent of scholars have an average follower base nearly 700 times that of scholars in the bottom 50 percent and nearly 100 times that of scholars in the other 99 percent.

These findings call into question whether Twitter and similar technologies are the equalizing forces they are sometimes portrayed to be. In this research, we also found a strong positive relationship between follower counts and number of tweets posted: the more tweets posted, the greater the followers one would expect to see. And a wide range of variables might mediate the number of tweets posted: it could be that extroverts tweet more than introverts, that people who find writing easy tweet more often than others, that scholars with family responsibilities have less time to tweet than those without, or that scholars in regions with robust smartphone data plan availability post more often than others. Inequities, in terms of participation and commanding attention and audience, are evident and go beyond digital skills and competencies.

Conclusion

Recognizing that online social networks are areas in which inequities exist is significant. While networks have been shown to allow scholars (junior and senior alike) to contribute to public knowledge creation and dissemination in ways that academic institutions do not necessarily manage, it is also important to recognize that networks circulate their own set of dominant voices. These voices may differ from those that circulate within the institutional hierarchy of academia, but may nonetheless constitute a sort of echo chamber. Additionally, because networks accord so much dominance to a few powerful voices, they may in fact be less evenly distributed or equal than institutional models of participation.

9

NETWORKS OF DISCLOSURE

The overwhelming majority of the research on social media and online networks has focused on how students, faculty members, and scholars in general use these technologies in teaching, learning, research, and outreach. Little attention has been paid to how these technologies are used by academics to care for one another and to disclose deeply personal or professional struggles (e.g., mental health issues). Why do scholars share struggles/vulnerabilities they are facing on social media? Have scholars benefited from such sharing? Have scholars experienced care, broadly conceived, through social media as a result of such sharing? If so, how do scholars care for one another using social media?

Care, Community, and Kindness

Online social networks can be viewed as places where scholars congregate to build ties, bonds, and solidarity, even when they may have not met each other face-to-face. Shared interests, causes, or values bring academics together. Some faculty and students also feel isolated at their universities and seek community and support online (Wesely, 2013; Ford, Veletsianos, & Resta, 2014). Although networked participation is not without drawbacks, for many scholars online social networks function as a parallel, or "shadow," academy where collegiality is present.

Online scholarly networks may enable community without subjecting participants to the never-ending array of performance metrics currently in use in higher education (Burrows, 2012) or the pressure to be productive with no end in sight (Shahjahan, in press). Mewburn and Thompson's (2013) analysis of blogs suggests that scholars may go online to find community and not necessarily to increase citations. In Stewart's (in press) study of networked scholars, appreciation for the care and community afforded by networked connections was highly visible.

The role of care and community in the contemporary academy is fraught. While an ethic of care has been documented to exist in a number of educational contexts (e.g., Borup, Graham, & Velasquez, 2013), academia's uncomfortable relationship with care is evident in many of its foundational processes:

> The careerist self-promotion that plagues our (every?) field renders relationships among colleagues – what used to be called (how quaint the phrase seems now!) the "community of scholars" – sometimes adversarial, often disingenuous and utilitarian. Nowhere is this degraded state of affairs more obvious than in the sphere of knowledge production, structured as it is by the processes and procedures of scholarly publication. …While many, and possibly most, scholars may claim they take into account their students' feelings, apparently other scholars' students are a different matter, at least when they submit articles for possible publication, especially when reviewers' aggression is made anonymous by the tradition of the "blind review." While emotional considerations of course ought not mute debate, surely they must influence the terms of debate – that is, if we are to debate pedagogically, how can we teach those we have alienated?
>
> *(Pinar, 2005, p. 266)*

Contemporary academia is increasingly a climate of narrowing academic opportunity (Clawson, 2009; MacFarlane, 2011). The trends toward contingent academic labour and rationalization of scholarship through narrow performance metrics have created an environment and culture wherein, as Pinar illustrates pointedly above, care is often mere rhetoric. Institutional concepts and enactments of care may not truly include contingent faculty or graduate students or others who fall outside the prestige economy of academic hiring. These individuals may find greater opportunity to both practice and experience care within the "shadow academy" of networked scholarly environments.

A culture of sharing is increasingly visible online, and in such sharing we often find examples of individuals (a) disclosing challenges and vulnerabilities, and (b) caring for one another. This may in part be easier within the shadow academy because of the ways in which the personal and the professional are collapsed, to greater or lesser extents, within social media networks (Sugimoto et al., 2015). The fact that social media allow people to form connections around points of common interest across geographic barriers (Tufekci, 2012) may also be key; many scholars are isolated specialists within their faculties and SNS offer them opportunities to build productive and even collaborative connections on a day-to-day basis with peers. These connections and collaborations may enable many otherwise junior or contingent scholars to be active participants and even leaders in their fields. Stewart (2015b) reports that all scholars in her ethnographic study "appeared to be engaged in curating and contributing resources to a broader 'conversation' in their field or area of interest rather than merely promoting themselves or their work ... open scholars may value scholarly networked participation as a means of building ties, accessing resources, and contributing to broader conversations" (p. 11).

Examples of academics expressing care and sharing examples of care with each other can be found in the open on social networks as well as in research studies. The Academic Kindness Tumblr blog, branded as "a record of unsolicited kindness, unexpected goodwill, and excessive generosity in academia" showcases a number of examples in which scholars have cared for one another.

One poster writes,

> While in the depths of maternity leave, I received an unsolicited and unexpected email from a very senior scholar in my field, whose work I admire, but with one of whose articles I had taken slight issue in my first book. The academic in question, whom I had never met, had nonetheless emailed to say how much she had enjoyed my book, was recommending it to her students, and hoped we'd meet some day to talk about our interests. I nearly didn't go back into academia after maternity leave, but the breathtaking generosity of this email was one of the reasons I did. Years later, I met this kind person, and she turned out to be as charming and generous in person as she was in that email.
>
> *(Griffin, n.d.)*

A second poster noted:

> I received an email from a senior scholar in my field. He had only just got to a published article of mine, and was writing to say how much he enjoyed it, and how much it extends the discourse. I'm currently going through the mill on the job market, and this short email (received on a Saturday morning) really re-established my confidence in myself and my scholarship. ... I replied, thanked him, and told him about my future research plans. This kind email turned into a lengthy exchange in which he offered detailed and helpful advice.
>
> *(Anonymous, n.d.)*

These examples of academic support and kindness – care for one another – were expressed via email. I have observed scholars caring for one another in online networks as well.

Michael Barbour, a professor at Sacred Heart University in Connecticut, is a scholar who has supported and cared for doctoral students over the years, as evidenced in his blog. Dr. Barbour's research has examined K–12 online education and, as a result of his expertise on the topic, he receives emails from students asking for feedback on their research efforts. Some of these emails have been published on his blog, accompanied with the advice that he has offered.

The demonstrations of support and solidarity that I've seen have taken place via comments (e.g., blog comments of encouragement) and via retweeting/reblogging practices. Such practices are oftentimes gestures of support and care because they serve to share an individual's writings/thoughts on a larger and broader scale, in effect amplifying their voice.

Networked scholarship and open scholarship interact in significant ways, and it appears that open practices (e.g., the creation of open content, the teaching of open courses, and so on) may also reflect a form of caring. For example, Couros (2009, ¶ 4) notes that open teachers advocate for *gift cultures*, which is a term used to refer to sharing or giving without an expectation of anything in return, potentially leading to a gift economy being developed that depends on "the paying-forward of interactions and meaningful collaborations." In other words, while a number of motives guide individuals' involvement in communities (Batson, Ahmad, & Tsang, 2002), gift economics, such as the ones that may be present in networked and open scholarship, depend on altruism and kindness.

Anonymity and Transparency

The place of anonymity in networked scholarship is complex. Identity-based platforms such as Twitter, Facebook, and blogs tend to dominate networked scholarship, as opposed to anonymous sites such as YikYak, which is a smartphone application that allows people to contribute posts to a location-based stream. While scholars can participate online on social media under long-standing pseudonyms, and build network ties and credibility through their pseudonymous participation, academic influence and careers tend to be tied to verifiable, public names. Thus, the professional benefits of circulating one's name and work in scholarly networks accrue primarily to named accounts. Yet the freedom of expression that anonymity affords means that there are a significant number of anonymous accounts and sites that deal with academic issues. Some would argue that sites which allow anonymous participation enable the spread of unsubstantiated and sometimes inflammatory information. Others would counter that anonymous participation enables greater transparency about the operations of power within higher education than named accounts do. There is evidence to support both of these perspectives.

The issues raised by anonymity and transparency in online social networks have been brought to broad cultural attention in recent years through the activities of Anonymous and Wikileaks. Wikileaks is a whistleblowing initiative that has gathered and released confidential and classified documents about the foreign policy activities of various state entities. Anonymous is a loosely-connected network of hacker activists who engage in vigilante publicity within networked publics, particularly related to individuals and events that status quo power systems appear to protect. Both of these initiatives emphasize enhancement of transparency in relation to issues that they deem significant, even though the legal standing of many of their activities is questionable. Both utilize digital technologies and networked connections to unearth information and make public and transparent what they believe should not be concealed by those in power. The relative anonymity that digital technologies can afford to speech acts enables members of both networks to operate without the same direct and personal consequences that they might face if they were to say the same things openly. However, some members of both Wikileaks and Anonymous have had their identities outed and have faced prosecution.

While academia does not – as far as I am aware – have an organized anonymous network of whistleblowers, the aims of transparency and speaking truth to power that undergird the Wikileaks and Anonymous manifestos is one that we find in networked scholars' practices as well. In fact, Kimmons (2014) argues that one of the characteristics shared by *all* emergent forms of scholarship is transparency. He writes that "[t]ransparency plays a role in these practices … as information is diffused freely and scholars' relationships, thoughts, opinions, and interactions take an increasingly public stage, thereby opening more aspects of their lives to both scrutiny and celebration."

The trend toward transparency reveals itself in a variety of networked scholarly practices. In relation to teaching, some scholars make their syllabi and activities public. In relation to research, some scholars make their data available to others. Scholars have also sought to make various heretofore esoteric practices more visible. Take the example of the Narrating Lives video project, wherein individuals were asked "to record short video responses to questions about their experiences as readers, scholars, and teachers." Or, the Paper Rejection Repository, which hosts rejection letters and reviewers' comments in relation to papers that were eventually published, in an attempt to demystify the process. The project's creator writes: "Rather than hiding these low points in the trajectory of a scientific paper, this forum offers a place to publish these letters and comments to educate others." Other quests seek to efficiently coalesce information in order for the contributing network to benefit from it. The Adjunct Project is one example of an initiative in which networks of scholars have formed to make visible the dire pay and working conditions facing precariously-employed faculty. In this project, scholars contributed information pertaining to their working conditions across institutions throughout the United States, providing evidence of what it is like to work in higher education in these positions.

Some of these initiatives and artifacts are eponymous or named, such as the tenure and promotion package submitted by Jon Becker, a professor at Virginia Commonwealth University, and made public through his networks. Many other efforts and activities, however, are anonymously posted: anonymous accounts are, and have always been, present within circles of networked scholarship. Named accounts can create risks for scholars who choose to disclose any issues or challenges that may be culturally perceived as expressions of vulnerability, since what they share will be tied to and searchable under their public, professional

identities. In networked scholarship, transparency tends to be focused less on the individual speaking than on the information and systems revealed in the process. Information that might reflect negatively on institutions and processes of higher education, such as the narratives shared within The Adjunct Project outlined above, allow for a raw examination of precariousness in academia precisely by protecting the identities of those speaking, who might otherwise face censure or loss of their already limited livelihoods.

The use of anonymity to raise challenging issues within higher education can also be seen on Reddit, the site described in chapter 4. One discussion thread was initiated by an individual who went by the username ripoffedu. While it was not clear if this person was an academic, his/her aim was to expose various practices and realities occurring in the for-profit education venture that employed him/her at the time (Reddit, n.d.). The author prefaced the discussion by stating, "I work for a for-profit education company. There are a few things I have to get off my chest … the industry is a complete joke and I'm sickened by what we do." In this case, we see that his/her ability to be anonymous, enabled him/her to be transparent in a way that identified speech might not have.

Disclosure

Anonymity and transparency also manifest in networked research processes. In May 2015, my colleague Bonnie Stewart and I sought to learn more about acts of online disclosure by scholars by interviewing a group of them about their experiences with disclosure, vulnerability, and care. We posted invitations for scholars to participate in our research, and also used email to invite specific individuals we knew had disclosed various personal and professional challenges they were facing. Our consent form read:

> We would like to invite you to participate to a study entitled Academics' use of social media: care and vulnerability. The purpose of this research is to describe, understand, and interpret academics' experiences with social media and in particular to explore how academics use social media to share the challenges they face, express their vulnerabilities, and experience care online.

As noted above, anonymity in networks is a complex issue that may sometimes enable greater freedom than named speech does. As with all other research projects, our ethics approval detailed the rights of the participants and the steps that we would take to protect their identity. One of the pillars of the research process and ethics is participant privacy and confidentiality. Various identifying details are often protected and care is taken to reduce the possibility that participants can be identified inadvertently or purposefully. Pseudonyms are often used, but also various other identifying details are anonymized. For instance, research focusing on Macalester College in St. Paul, Minnesota might allude to the institution as a "liberal arts college in the Midwest." Or, a participant's age might be changed from a specific age (e.g., 33) to an age range (e.g., 30–40 years old). This was the first project I've been involved in that required participants to recall and share life experiences that may have been painful or traumatic, and Bonnie and I took extra care in trying to ensure that participants were comfortable sharing their experiences with us.

Yet, while we initially sought anonymous participation from networked scholars, our focus on already publicly enacted narratives of disclosure opened up new and interesting intersections of citation, participation, and collaboration. As it turned out, the vast majority of the individuals who participated in the disclosure research project elected to be identified openly. Perhaps because most of the participants who made themselves available to us had already made the decision to disclose the topic of their interviews on public platforms, many determined that anonymity made no sense in their particular cases. Others noted that networked scholars to some extent inhabit public intellectual roles, and thus they felt that to own and honour their disclosures, they needed to attach a public name and identity to them, to counter cultural shame biases. Thus, in the interviews I present below to explore disclosures made by scholars online, I use their real names, as they requested. There are other participants in our research whose original disclosures were anonymous or who have elected to speak to us anonymously, in order to enable greater transparency and disclosure without fear of reprisal. In those cases, our research artifacts use pseudonyms of the participants' choosing.

Overall, we found that scholars define and relate to the concept of disclosure in a wide variety of ways. Scholars make both professional and personal disclosures in public in online social networks; some share news related to family or health issues, some share challenges related to work or professional status. Some disclosures may sit at the intersection of the personal and professional, as when a contingent faculty member requires health or bereavement leave, or when a scholar worries that disclosure of a mental health condition may impact employability. People may choose to disclose differently on different platforms, depending on the degree to which audiences on those platforms are perceived to fall into personal or professional circles. Some people may write about their challenges with academic, analytic remove; others from a more affective point of view.

The challenges that scholars face in academia are well documented. Academic hierarchies are sites of power that may shape individuals' experiences according to their rank. Keashly and Neuman (2010) for example, found that faculty-faculty bullying tends to be indirect, and that tenured faculty tend to use direct forms of aggression to less powerful individuals (e.g., untenured faculty, staff) and indirect forms of aggression toward individuals with the same or more power (e.g., other tenured faculty, senior administrators). These experiences tend to be difficult to address within institutions, and networks may provide an outlet for disclosing and exploring academic aggressions and their effects. A number of scholars for example, have anonymously disclosed instances of professional abuse and cruelty to a Tumblr blog called *Academia Is Killing My Friends*, wherein they described cases of depression, anxiety, and self harm. One anonymous poster wrote: "Over a year ago I told my supervisors I was suicidally depressed. They told me not to worry because you couldn't tell from my work. Then none of us ever mentioned it again." Some scholars also utilize networks to talk about the ways in which race, gender, and disability issues intersect with their experiences of the academy.

In our research, we found that public disclosures shared on social media often had to do with personal rather than professional challenges. For example, Alec Couros wrote a deeply moving blog post about the passing of his father, and has shared his memories of his father on social media. His blog post says:

> My dad died suddenly on March 26, 2013. I have about a dozen, half-written blog posts on my computer that I just can't bring myself to publish. Some of these posts describe the life of my dad, and others are my conversations with him after his death. None of these posts feel right. None of these posts are good enough to describe his life, his accomplishments, his lasting influence on me, or how horribly I miss him. He was my father and my very best friend. And his loss is so incredibly painful … But I have to move on. By writing a few incomplete thoughts here I am hoping that I can move forward in some little way. I know that dad would want that.
>
> *(Couros, 2013)*

In his interview with us, he described his decision to share this event and responses he received as a result of his sharing.

Interviewer: Was [the death of your father] one of the first times that you had shared something that intensely personal, yet difficult?

Alec: Absolutely … it's really the most tragic event that I've ever shared in any media.

Interviewer: Could you share with me your decision to share it? Was there even a question of "do I share this" and "do I share this now?"

Alec: It didn't feel foreign at all. It felt like part of the process … my hundred thousandth tweet was the birth of my youngest son … When you get into that mode of announcing those big life moments, it didn't make any sense not to announce this [the death of my dad] … Once I posted it, I didn't look at it. I don't think I looked at it for a week … yet it felt like something I had to do. Pick up a casket, post on social media. It's very much part of the grieving process. I've never had anyone else that close to me pass so I can't

> *compare* it to what mourning would have looked like. This never happened to me in the 1990s.
>
> It didn't seem odd or strange. At least no explicit part of me felt that I needed to do it for comfort or support but I'm sure there's some other level … many of the responses talked about their own deaths and their own fathers passing. Still, when I continue to post those things, it's very common for those posts, people to reach out and through their mourning they touch out to yours and they touch you through those shared experiences of having been through that.

Scholars also share health crises and the resultant identity shifts and experiences in networked spaces, inviting support and also awareness of particular issues. Our research project included scholars who had written about both mental and physical health issues, and navigated significant identity challenges and shifts in public. One participant, Becky Hogue, noted that disclosures can allow scholars to open up complex identity conversations and connections that institutional identity categories do not necessarily enable.

Becky had maintained a blog as a PhD candidate and educational technology professional, but opened a new blogging space when diagnosed with breast cancer. When she went to her first academic conference after treatment, she found it interesting to analyze how the long-term disclosure process had made her more intimately connected to academic connections who had nonetheless engaged with her and offered care through her cancer journey:

> Maybe it's just because I'm more of a person (to others). So I have more of that presence than I did before, and so with that, there is more of a connection, I guess … really what I have noticed and felt in the last three-four months, has been a deepening of connections, where things just really, were much more in-depth. And we have personal conversations, and that's sort of one of those things that happened at (the conference), was having those personal conversations that I otherwise wouldn't have had with people based on just my other identity 'cause there wasn't enough of me.

Becky noted in the interview that online disclosures can have an impact not only on professional audiences and connections, but closer to home. Family and friends may be uncomfortable with a loved one's choice to open up publicly about challenges and may struggle with the boundaries of self-presentation chosen by that loved one. Thus the risks of disclosing personal and professional challenges are not limited to professional repercussions, but may create tensions or heartache at home.

Interviewer: How do you present yourself?

Becky: On the breast cancer blog, I try to be very authentic, and it was a very conscious decision early on, but sometimes not an easy one for my family. I had to warn them that part of the issue is that I'm doing it [the act of blogging about cancer] an injustice if I am not authentic, which means that I need to deal honestly when I'm having issues with depression or anxiety, or mental health issues, as well as physical health issues, or a bad day. Those things are real, and … if I was sugar-coating things, I wasn't going to be authentic. It becomes a big challenge for a lot of women that are writing in that experience, because they feel the need to protect people within their family and communities and kids and all of this, and so they are very guarded. And since I didn't really have as much to risk in that area, I guess I felt safer to be able to put that out.

Social media participation seems to demand the construction of legible identities, and thus opens the door to some forms of identity disclosure. Jen Jack, a queer and trans scholar, explored the ways in which social media bios and identity profiles allow identities to be disclosed – or at least signalled – visibly.

Jen Jack: The blog, you're supposed to have a photo of yourself, and you land on this page, and it'll look pretty gay. And then, there is my gender which uses s/he. So, it's like, "Who are you?" right away. "Oh, you're trans. Her name is Jen Jack. Okay." That's very, very clear. On Twitter, it says what am I interested in? I'm interested in queer-trans life. I am. I study it. I also happen to be queer and trans. There are very few people who study trans life that aren't psychologists … Everyone who's trans is studying trans life. I don't know many people that aren't. Or they're dating someone who is, so they're queer in that way. Otherwise, there'd be a psychologist studying in like a …

Interviewer: In an outside kind of way?

Jen Jack: A "their life is so hard" way, yeah. Another population at risk … Then, there's a picture of me on Twitter, and I look really gay, and I'm always talking about gay stuff, and I'm Tweeting about gay stuff, and I'm blogging for Huffington Post about gay stuff. I'm just really gay. I don't mention I'm a trans person, but if I'm gonna use the pronouns I want, it makes me trans."

Experiences of Care

In our research, we were also interested in understanding how care and social media interacted. One of our questions focused on the reactions that social media posts elicited. We asked informants to describe to us how others reacted to their post and to share with us whether and how they experienced concern, interest, consideration, or care.

Becky Hogue, as noted above, disclosed her breast cancer diagnosis. She reported to us that she was careful to frame her disclosure in ways that allowed people to express care, but that she was nonetheless surprised at where the care came from.

Becky: I gave a way for people to help. Quite often, people want to help, but they don't know how. And so, I made it easy. I said, "Send me a postcard." It's an easy way to say, "Hey, I'm thinking of you" ... there's some new empathy cards out which are awesome.

What really surprised me was the number of people from around the world that made a difference. And this is actually something that brought M [another academic] and I closer, because she's actually one of the early people ... When I found out that for certain I was going to have chemotherapy, I reached out to her right away, 'cause I wanted head scarves. And she's the person that I knew would appreciate what it means to wear a head scarf ... and the reality check is, where she lives, you can buy a head scarf for very little, where here, they cost a fortune ... and something that they do that I didn't know is that it's actually common to share scarves [in that culture]. So, with a close friend, you would give them a scarf that was yours, which is different than buying one.

Interviewer: Yes, okay.

Becky: Yeah. And so, and she sent me a couple scarves that were hers. I sent her a scarf that I bought in Turkey. And so, that exchange happened, in part, because of that sort of reaching out.

But what was interesting is that my face-to-face colleagues, for the most part, disengaged ... Some of my face-to-face friends actually have reached out and become closer through this process, and have connected through the process. But then others just totally disconnected. And where I really noticed the disconnect more than anywhere else is with my academic colleagues. Now, in part, it's a face-to-face program primarily, and I'm not there all the time, so that when I am there, people would make that effort to do something. But, I've put out there a couple times, "Anyone want to go to breakfast on Friday?" or "Anyone want to go to dinner on Thursday?" and other than one or two people that I connect closely with, everyone else is like not interested.

Interviewer: That's a shame.

Becky: And so, it's sort of like this whole dispersion of networks that has happened, and it's not at all how I expected it to be. ... Maybe it's the type of people that are drawn to social media, the people that I met, my online connections became deeper, right? And there ... That's where the care came.

We also talked about care with Richard Hall, a UK academic who shared a post documenting and exploring his own personal struggle with depression and anxiety during years of what academia would term peak productivity in a scholar's life. In it, he addresses and repudiates the stereotype of the "lazy depressive," challenging societal assumptions about mental health.

Richard: There is no redemption or salvation. Except from the blackness and the bleakness. But there is the on-going search for solidarity with myself, and through that a solidarity with other people. The search for my own humanity. And the recognition that in getting up and in going to work, and in managing a team, and in working co-operatively, and in writing, and in speaking, that I might recognise the courage it takes to stop doing stuff and just be. To stop and to find faith in me.

That my route away from crippling depression lies in my caring for me.

And this is an on-going battle that will end with my ability to cope with a few emotional problems. To learn to like and love and find faith in myself. And in you, too.

Richard reported a real outpouring of care as the result of his post.

Richard: I got loads of text messages from people that I know and love, or kinda far and wide really. Yeah I would like to say when I woke up in the morning, there was a phenomenal number of text messages. There were a phenomenal number of comments on Facebook that were just like really ... that went from the "Oh my god, I never knew" through to the "I don't know where you find the kinda strength" through to "You're an amazing role model, and I'm really proud to know you," and all of that. Do you know what I mean?

Interviewer: That's great.

Richard: And then somebody says. ... And then there's D saying "I hope. ... You've got 56 comments here, I hope you're reading them. I hope you can save them all" kinda stuff.

Interviewer: Is there any one memorable response that you received that stands out, or powerful response that you received? And why does it stand out, if it does?

Richard: No, I can't actually. It's interesting. It's kind of ... From J's "Well of course we know this, Richard. Everyone knows this. And we still love you" ... through to D's kind of pragmatic "Look at how much love there is on this space for you," through ... I think H left a message sorta saying just that she'd read it. She read it in tears three times in an airport waiting for a plane. And it's those things I think that just kinda ... that stay. Yeah, it's those things that stay.

Interviewer: Did it give you a sense that you had made a difference in other people's conversations with themselves even?

Richard: Well I'll tell you what's interesting: there's a friend at work who said to me, "I read that, Richard. How are you gonna explain this to your team?" I manage a team of seven people. So it's kinda "How you're gonna manage that? What are they gonna think now?" And I kinda thought "Well I'm hoping that they think. ... Because I talked to them around 2012, when my mum was ill and when we were nursing my mum, October, November 2012. I had to have six weeks off work with depression and anxiety, and it's just like too much. Yeah I used that as an example with my team, when one or two of them have had to have little bits ... not loads of time, a little bit of time-off. And I've been able to sorta say "Look, I'm not superhuman. If you remember, this stuff happened too. ... And we're still here, and we're still implementing these things. And we're still doing these things, and we're still keeping on, keeping on."

Sometimes, the same online platforms can generate criticism along with care. When scholars disclose challenges that are primarily professional in nature, or when they disclose online to broad public audiences outside personally cultivated channels, they sometimes experience responses that are less than supportive of their risks. Hierarchy and power challenges, as noted earlier, can be endemic in academic environments, thus addressing these issues can open scholars to vehement denials and attacks. Likewise, openly challenging the growing norm of precarious employment in higher education in public can amplify the vulnerability of that position rather than result in care.

Lee Skallerup Bessette, now in an alternative academic career in higher education, wrote extensively about adjunct and contingent employment issues during her years as a "trailing spouse" in higher education, and eventually gained wide visibility and readership as a regular columnist in *Inside Higher Ed*. Yet her posts disclosed a frustration with the system and with her situation that some readers of *Inside Higher Ed* felt the need to censure, even though the same posts simultaneously built her a network of friends and supporters. She found that expressing vulnerability could be an unpleasant experience, particularly in media comments.

> *Lee:* There's still a lot of stigma, right? It's all the things we're not supposed to talk about, it's all of the things we're not supposed to admit. I mean, part of me was also thinking about the people … the concern trolls who in the past were all asking me about my mental health and all of these kinds of things when I was talking about being an adjunct or talking about being the trailing spouse. Even when I got back in the classroom, still being dissatisfied with the way that the structure worked out, then people who were just like, "Well, just suck it up." Or just, "Maybe there's something wrong."

Lee noted that disclosing and exploring her own precarious employment in spite of the risks to her own professional image was nonetheless cathartic and sparked expressions of care:

> *Lee:* If you go back into the early archives [of my writing on *Inside Higher Ed*] … there was a lot of anger there against, not just being an adjunct, but the entire system … how it was all a scam. You know what I mean? One of my biggest ones that put me on the map was the one that I did with University of Venus, for *Inside Higher Ed*, called, "How Higher Ed Makes Most Things Meaningless." And that was not just about contingency, but it was about writing online, doing other things, being, I think, in the now. But really, what I was getting at was just like, we can do all these things, the public scholars, but none of it counts.
>
> And so that was … it was pretty incendiary, too, I think. There was always writing from that perspective, from my perspective on that, and this is just five years later. I'm just … I try to be more thoughtful about it, I guess. But, yes (it did generate) a lot of care and a lot of solidarity. … And I'm thinking that that's really what … why I wanted to write it was because I knew I wasn't alone in that sort of sense, I knew that. I knew that I wasn't the only one going through these kinds of things. It was my way of using a larger platform too, not just to work through my own stuff, but to also show … you are also not alone.

Overall, while not all scholars who participated in the project had received overt expressions of care as a result of social media disclosures, the majority reported that the capacity to self-publish disclosures and to target particular platforms or audiences was an enabling factor in encouraging them to share challenges. Others like Lee also noted that they felt an impetus, as public scholars, to talk about issues and help open up conversations that otherwise might be difficult for others to have or engage with.

Conclusion

In the end, social media functions as a place where academics can make disclosures and make themselves vulnerable, if they choose. Social media disclosures also provide opportunities and vehicles for scholars to express and experience care.

Intimate disclosures, and disclosures in general, are fascinating aspects of scholars' lives online, but have yet to receive the scholarly attention they deserve. Whether going online to find a supportive community in the face of an academic environment seen as oppressive, or venting about day-to-day challenges, or finding solace in sharing a difficult situation, scholars' reasons for disclosing their experiences are varied.

Above all, however, these narratives – narratives that we need more of – serve as powerful reminders that academic identities are intertwined with scholars' personal self-concepts in complex and intricate ways. In the next chapter, we are going to explore this idea further and investigate how the self that scholars present online is authentic, but simultaneously incomplete and fragmented.

10

FRAGMENTED NETWORKS

Do scholars represent themselves fully and in authentic ways when they are online? What aspects of their identity might they leave out? How do they choose which parts of their identity to disclose?

Becoming a Networked Scholar

I remember the exact moment when I decided to join Twitter and create a professional blog. I was reading chapter proposals for a book that I was editing, and one proposal made such a big impression upon me that I decided to invest more time in using networked technologies, beyond the parameters of the courses that I was teaching. At first, I often struggled with the notion of public participation on social media, of "putting myself out there," publishing draft ideas, and sharing details of my professional and non-professional life. Like many other scholars I have spoken with, I assumed that others would find my musings incomplete, dull, and irrelevant.

In retrospect, the source of this struggle was multifold. Social media platforms are designed to encourage individuals to share. Facebook's status update prompt asks: "What's on your mind?" My Twitter client prompts: "What's happening?" Part of my struggle as a newly-networked scholar was not wanting to be seen as bragging, or what one research informant called "humble bragging." He said: "I recently got an award, which I haven't shared online because I think it's too much of a humble brag … That feels weird sharing something where you've gotten an award." Part of my struggle was also the training and scholarly enculturation that I received during my graduate degree. This training, implicit as it may have been, highlighted the notion that researchers (a) can be "scooped out of ideas" if they share ideas prematurely and (b) are experts, knowledgeable in their field of study, confident of their work, and should present themselves as such.

Since then, I have learned that I am not the only scholar facing these struggles. Others have eloquently documented their own challenges with open sharing. Some have noted that publishing "half-baked" ideas can be a dangerous career move for scholars because, even though the individual might benefit from thinking through ideas via writing, others may judge the shared work in a decontextualized manner without necessarily observing or understanding how particular blog entries, for example, are situated within larger scholarly conversations or within an idea's broader evolution over time. As we have already seen, scholars also struggle with the degree to which they should share professional and non-professional information. These issues point to an increasing tension between personal and professional identity, the spectrum of sharing that lies between the two, and perceptions of who a scholar is and what s/he does. Sharing and issues pertaining to whether scholarly identity is distinct from non-professional identity permeate social media participation.

Admittedly, identity issues permeate contemporary scholarship more broadly. In discussing the tattoos of faculty members for example, Leonard (2012, ¶ 6) notes that "[i]n a university culture, where faculty are often reduced to numbers – grant dollars, student credit hours, teaching-evaluation scores, publication numbers – tattoos offer a space to disentangle our individual selves from the bureaucratic and corporate university." In the same way, the social media uses that I've seen in my ethnographic journey often centre around issues of identity.

The presentation of the academic self online is influenced by a variety of factors. As we see above, social media exerts pressure to share more. Scholars may also be reflective and uncertain about what to share and how much to share. What seems increasingly evident to me is that what scholars reveal online about themselves is influenced by professional issues, collapsed contexts, imagined and invisible audiences, and identity work. What scholars reveal online about themselves is neither fully authentic nor fully performative. Scholars' presentation of self online appears to be fragmented, consciously constructed, and socially shaped.

The Fragmented Educator

The phrase *fragmented networks* centres on the notion that scholars' digital identities are fragmented. This understanding stems from a study Royce Kimmons and I conducted with a group of educators (Kimmons & Veletsianos, 2014) and serves as the foundation of the understanding that scholars' expression of identity online is fragmented.

Given that direct links exist between online and offline identities (boyd, 2008; Coiro, Knobel, Lankshear, & Leu, 2008) and that participation in social spaces is connected to identity in significant ways (Gee, 2009; Ivanič, 1998), Kimmons and I suspected that individuals' sense of who they are – their identities – are impacted by the factors that shape how people participate on social media. Our definition of identity stemmed from Lemke and Van Helden (2009) who described authentic identities as "highly adaptable constellations of identifications and affiliations" (p. 153). Thus, we studied how a group of pre-service teachers viewed their developing identities within social networking sites and developed a framework to describe this phenomenon. We conducted interviews with 18 individuals. Fifteen of these individuals completed a second interview and 11 participated in focus groups. Our analysis revealed that participants shaped their participation in ways that they deemed to be "appropriate" to their social media audiences; most viewed their participation as a direct expression of who they were, yet felt that their participation only represented a small fragment of who they truly were. The framework that arose from that study suggests that, for these individuals, online participation consists of sharing pieces of themselves that they believe are acceptable to others ("acceptable identity fragments"), which are each "intentional, authentic, transitional, necessarily incomplete, and socially-constructed and -responsive." This finding departs from previous literature in one significant way: in contrast to Goffman's (1959) dramaturgical view that views people as "acting" to convey particular impressions, participants in this research insisted that they were always themselves. Rather than "acting," participants were *revealing* parts of themselves. But these parts were always only facets of self rather than any more overarching sense of self.

The Fragmented Scholar

Based on the research described above, I propose that scholars' presentation of self online is conscientious, fragmented and socially-constructed. I draw on a number of studies to support this argument.

The ability to create, manage, and traverse profiles on social networking sites has given rise to digital notions of self-presentation and impression formation. Researchers have argued that scholars need to be intentional in creating and managing their web presence (Lowenthal & Dunlap, 2012), and many how-to books and manuals exist to inform scholars how to participate effectively and efficiently on social media. However, there are other ways to view the presentation of the self online, and Stewart (2012) sees six key selves in social media, or six ways of being: the performative or public self; the quantified or articulated self; the asynchronous self; the polysocial or augmented reality self; and the neo-liberal or branded self. These perspectives of the self can be further divided in two groups: the self that scholars create/manage and the self that is created/structured for them.

The consciously-constructed self, or the one that is intentionally created, presented, and managed by individual scholars, is a topic that I explored in my analysis of 45 scholars' tweets described in chapter 4. I found that when scholars use Twitter, they often draw attention to their work and professional endeavors. Below are some examples of tweets highlighting lectures/presentations and interviews that scholars gave:

- Heading to [University Name] to give a talk to the [name] Group: [URL]
- Appreciative for the comments and the hundreds of views/day on this presentation: [URL].
- In my interview with the editor of [name], I discuss [topic]: [URL]
- [URL]: My interview on [topic related to professional interests]
- Interview with [Periodical name]: [URL]

Tweets that highlight colleague achievements ("Enjoyed @user's response to [topic]: [URL]"), institutional events/successes ("Well done [Name] for accepting a position at [University and Department] [URL]"), and appreciation ("great colleagues @user1 @user2 @user3") can be seen as laudatory, but also as actions and information that manage impressions. Such "public displays of connection" are said to validate status and connection identity (Donath & boyd, 2004). In her study of networked scholars, Stewart (in press) found that "credited parties consistently retweeted credit-giving tweets more often than other forms of attention directed at them, indicating that sharing the praise of others may, like humor and self-deprecation, constitute acceptable attention–cultivation in networks" (p. 14).

The analysis of scholars' tweets also found that, outside of their professional practices and presentations, scholars additionally drew attention to their personal accomplishments. One common practice related to individuals snapping and sharing a photograph a day as a way to document their lives, enhance their photography skills, and learn about each other. When a participant tweeted, "Shot and posted pictures every single day for #SnapAPicToday. See them here: [URL]," not only was she sharing information related to her interests, but she was also highlighting personal characteristics such as tenacity and dedication. Dayter's (2014) investigation of self-praise in a community of practice, which found that socially acceptable forms of praise were contingent upon the norms of the community to which they were directed, might suggest that tenacity and dedication are characteristics perceived positively among scholars.

The activities identified in the examples above present scholars as individuals who take on public intellectual roles and willingly and knowingly share information about themselves and their practice. Yet why would they share such information? What goals do these activities fulfill? Are scholars' altruistically sharing information for the benefit of the communities to which they belong? Or is information–sharing a self-serving activity? Are scholars sharing information in order to assist the profession to grow intellectually, or are they attempting to develop a "brand" around themselves? To what extent are scholars' impression management activities, as signified by such things as the content of their tweets or references to other individuals in the profession, aimed at projecting an idealized scholar to audiences? Here we are returning to Goffman's (1959) dramaturgical perspective, where we might say that scholars "act" to convey a particular impression. From the fragmented scholars perspective though, we can also say that scholars are revealing aspects of themselves in a controlled way.

It appears that scholars engage in online participation and expressions of identity in ways that they deem appropriate to specific contexts or acceptable to the specific relationships they have with others in that context. This may not necessarily differ entirely from the ways in which they participate and express themselves in other, offline social contexts.

For example, many scholars may see themselves in the words of Jane, a mid-career scholar: "I manage my relationship with my family, parenting, close relationships with people who aren't online very differently; professionally I'm different, and in interpersonal settings, I'm very quiet. The person [that I present] is authentic but I withhold a lot." In other words, Jane highlights that she is putting forward fragments of her authentic self, and believes that her online participation is not fully representative of who she is, though it is genuine.

Chris, another mid-career scholar, is more explicit in the types of things that he will not share on the social media sites he frequents. With regard to his online participation, he says,

> [I]t doesn't capture me on the weekends with some of my closest friends doing the things we would have done in high school. It doesn't capture me, the card counter, that goes to the casino and has done that professionally since 2007. It doesn't capture the frustrations I have with my children or family.

Even though Chris notes that he aims "for a fairly authentic representation" of himself on these platforms, his uses of the platform align with fragments of his life and thus those fragments are the ones addressed in his social media presentation.

Mary also indicates that her online participation is not fully representative, and that in face-to-face encounters, she is "a real introvert, and you can't tell that – I don't think – on social media." She also highlights the relational nature of how identity is perceived when she says:

> While I was working full time in higher education, I couldn't afford for my students to see any news I might not want to put on a poster. Or for the staff who followed me either. So at that point I didn't make it clear where I worked, and my avatar was just reflections in mirrors. So, they couldn't see whether it was the boss or the Director of Higher Education or not. And I was very circumspect, and at that point in time, certainly when I first started using Twitter, I didn't tweet very much that was related to me personally. It was all academic stuff.

Mary's gradual expansion of her Twitter usage beyond strictly professional self-presentation appears to be relatively common among networked scholars, as scholarly Twitter communities tend, by example, to encourage some level of personal connection in addition to scholarly discussion. Even though another individual my colleagues and I interviewed believes that "it's different on each platform," and that she also is not fully representing herself online, of all the platforms that she uses, Twitter is the one that she finds most representative. She asserts,

> I think that the place that is most representative of me is probably Twitter, just because I share more interests, more varied interests on there … I share a lot of stuff about writing. I'm a big fan of documentary films, so I share a lot about that. And those don't always come through on Facebook or the blog … so more facets of me, but also not actually really personal … Still very curated and at a distance.

Likewise, LP describes that her expression of herself varies between platforms and audiences. While many scholars find value in using Twitter under their real names, she tweets under a pseudonym, to allow – in many of the ways explored in the chapter on disclosures – for a greater range of openness and transparency on topics and aspects of identity that do not correspond with professional societal norms. As she says, she attempts to express herself fully in one particular platform, but does so in an informed, guarded, and managed way.

LP: I am on Twitter, and I use Tumblr. And I have an account on LinkedIn. My LinkedIn account is a purely professional account that has my real name on it, with no links to Twitter, or websites or blogs or anything else. It's all 100% professional. And it is very streamlined, very, "These are the jobs I've had, this is the school I've gone to, this is the undergrad I went to, and these are my connections." And I'm not as active on LinkedIn yet, I'm trying to force myself to be more active on it because that's the professional networking place … So, very professional there, professional picture, no hobbies, none … I don't even put what I like to do in my free time.

Twitter, I kind of go back and forth. I'm very weird. At night, sometimes, I will lock my account, and I will put up pictures of myself and will have these sexual conversations, and I'll have just very open kinds of pictures. And then in the morning, before I unlock my account, I will go and delete things, images that I don't want people who are not in there to see. So I think generally, I have one kind of image on Twitter, but I turn it up a bit in Twitter After Dark.

I also very seriously curate my Twitter. I block people a lot. I un-follow people, I'm very, very serious about who I engage with, and who I allow into my Twitter space, because I am trying to keep it so that I can be fully myself. That's kind of the one place I can be fully myself, so I'm trying to keep it that way.

Interviewer: [It sounds like] you're at least finding ways to show aspects of who you are, to express aspects of who you are.

LP: I think my Twitter is probably about 95% or so representative of who I am … I really do feel safe on Twitter, relatively safe on Twitter. I would say the part that's left are the parts that aren't necessarily mine to share. I have relationships with people who have not agreed to be talked about on Twitter, and so there are parts of my life that I don't talk about at all in terms of relationships because the person I'm in a relationship with doesn't wanna be talked about on Twitter. And then my primary partner, who I live with, he's okay with being talked about on Twitter as long as I don't name. So I talk about him all the time. So, most of it is free, maybe 90–95% is … 95% of my life is on … Yeah.

Interviewer: And if I were … If I caught your Twitter in time when it was unlocked, what kind of impression would you want me to draw about you as a person?

LP: [chuckle] That I am very open-minded, and I believe in sexual autonomy for women. I am a woman-ist, I am a feminist, I am part of a kink community, happily. I love black men, I love black families. [chuckle] I have a family, and I adore them. And I am on Twitter to also help uplift other women … So I think those are the kinds of things that I would want you to see and recognize about me. And that I'm smart and educated, and trying to make a nice world for myself.

Can scholars' online expression of identity ever be fully representative of who they are?

Facebook and Twitter are both designed to prompt people to express their identities in particular directions, to particular audiences. However, as one scholar we interviewed argues, scholars' expressions of identity online may not ever fully be representative of who they are:

> I would say my question is, can it be [fully representative]? Can it really be? I mean, I think when you have to go out there and put yourself out there, you're obviously … You're going to choose and you're going to filter. And just by the time and activity and what you can do, it's not going to be entirely you. And I also say in the face-to-face basis, are you ever entirely you as you see yourself?

This especially rings true when considering what scholars share online and how the audiences they are connected with shape their sharing. Chris for example, noted that he shares what he believes would be interesting to his audience which is imagined to be "K–12 educators, pre-service teachers, higher ed … Hashtags I use, for instance, are edchat, highered, edtech – stuff in that area."

Conclusion

Scholars' participation on social media is fragmented: it is distributed across platforms, and even though it is actively created and curated, it is incomplete and not fully representative of who they are as people. Our relations with others, whether peers, family, or friends, also shape who we are and who we present to others online. danah boyd's reflection on the ways that audiences change and shape what we, as people, do and reveal, online is telling, and provides a summary for this chapter:

> I started blogging in 1997. I was 19 years old. I didn't call it blogging then, and my blog didn't look like it does now … I posted entries a few times a week as part of an independent study on Buddhism as a Brown University student … Each week, the monk I was working with would ask me to reflect on certain things, and I would write. And write. And write … I decided to type my thoughts and that, if I was going to type them, I might as well put them up online. Ah, teen logic. Most of those early reflections were deeply intense. I posted in detail about what it meant to navigate rape and abuse, to come into a sense of self in light of scarring situations. I have since deleted much of this material, not because I'm ashamed by it, but because I found that it created the wrong introduction. As my blog became more professional, people would flip back and look at those first posts and be like errr … uhh … While I'm completely open about my past, I've found that rape details are not the way that I want to start a conversation most of the time. So, in a heretical act, I deleted those posts. What my blog is to me and to others has shifted tremendously over the years. For the first five years, my blog was read by roughly four people. That was fine because I wasn't thinking about audience. I was blogging to think, to process, to understand. To understand myself and the world around me. I wasn't really aware of or interested in community building so I didn't really participate in the broader practice. Blogging was about me. Until things changed.
>
> *(boyd, 2014)*

11

SCHOLARLY NETWORKS, OR SCHOLARS IN NETWORKS?

In previous chapters, I argued that the majority of the research on scholars' digital and networked practices focuses on professional matters, and little effort is directed toward how people use these technologies to care for one another and to disclose matters that are deeply personal to them. I have also explained how scholars' expression of identity online is fragmented. These two findings together reflect a broader gap in the literature. In effect, research into open, digital, and social scholarship focuses predominantly on professional matters, and thus provides little insight into how scholars' lives intersect with social media, networks, and technology overall. To understand scholars' lives, we need to examine more than just their scholarly practices. We need to explore their activities, participation, and experiences with social media and networks in an expansive way that includes both their professional and non-professional ways of being. And, yes, that includes the pictures of the food they share.

What Do Scholars Eat for Breakfast?

The Academic Breakfast Tumblr blog was started in May 2014 as a networked project to gather photographs and descriptions of academics' breakfasts. Each blog post starts with a photograph of an individual's meal followed by a response to a set of standard questions, some of which are demographic and some of which are intended to describe the individual's breakfast and his/her philosophy of food. The creator of the project, Lucas Crawford, a faculty member at Simon Fraser University at the time, listed six reasons for the project. Crawford (2014, ¶ 2) wrote that this project was created to:

> remind ourselves that eating is a public matter ... see how food habits may differ across rank, region, nation, and gender ... test our hypotheses about

social class, precarious work, and food access … demystify academia by entering its intimate spaces and nourishing scenes … remember that academics are bodies … [and] produce an alternative aesthetic representation of academic life.

A quick glance at the tumblr site reveals participation from around the world, with scholars from New Zealand, Mexico, Scotland, and Slovenia all featured on the first page alone, in addition to North American contributions.

This project illustrates the fact that scholars' digital lives go beyond scholarship. They are intertwined with scholars' sense of self, and even though scholarly identity may be a defining characteristic of who scholars are, online activities don't end with scholarship. This project not only demystifies academia, but it also humanizes it, making visible the diversities and commonalities – coffee features heavily in the majority of posts – of how scholars feed their bodies and minds.

Living Social

Twitter is frequently dismissed as a platform of meaningless soliloquies and dull updates. Malesky and Peters (2012) assert that "many Tweets contain relatively mundane status updates or information about the Tweeter," and Hough (2009, p. 411) acknowledges that the service is "[o]ften ridiculed as a frothy time-waster." During his time as president of the University of British Columbia (UBC), Dr. Stephen Toope summarized his feelings about Twitter in an interview with UBC's student run newspaper, and highlighted many of the concerns that academics in particular may have with the platform:

I despise Twitter, truthfully. I think it's one of the worst things that's been created in my lifetime, and so there's no way I'm going to go on it. I dislike everything about it. I think that the notion of the immediate reaction to something without any reflection, the idea that you can say anything that matters in the limited number of characters you're given, and that you have to do it immediately, and everyone will respond immediately with no reflection, I think it's the worst of our society.

(Wakefield, 2013)

While Toope may be correct about the fact that Twitter limits the number of characters per message, the rest of his diatribe is more a reflection of cultural narratives about social media and minimally examined assumptions and prejudices about what people do on it. We can gain a more refined and informed perspective on scholars' engagement – and reflective processes – by examining the information that they post. For instance, in Veletsianos and Kimmons (2015), a project where we analyzed about 650,000 tweets from 469 scholars, we found that more than half of the tweets mentioned other users and about a quarter were replies to others.

In the data set of 4,500 tweets I used to investigate scholars' practices, I found that, without exception, all participants shared updates pertinent to their day-to-day activities. These updates might be construed to be meaningless chatter. However, they can also be seen as representing important personal and social commentary and identity signaling because they inform others of the sender's current activities, intentions, likes and dislikes, and life outside the profession. Rather than representing meaningless chatter, such updates introduce opportunities to explore shared interests, experiences, goals, mindsets, and life dispositions/aspirations; like water-cooler conversations in offline professional contexts, they serve as ways for individuals to form connections. More than 40% of the scholars in VanNoorden's (2014) *Nature* study indicated that they use Twitter specifically to discover peers, and Stewart's (2015b) study suggests that commonality is seldom defined by active Twitter users based on disciplinary interests alone. Thus, extra-curricular signals of identity serve a purpose that Toope should not dismiss. Scholars share information about matters that are important to them including their hobbies, relationships, beliefs, events, meals, and celebrations. Examples of such updates include the following:

- I am reading Gibson's Neuromancer tonight.
- I ♥ Hey Jude by the Beatles: [URL]
- Here is my latest artwork: [URL]
- My son and I are really excited to see my parents tomorrow.
- [Husband's name] and I are celebrating our 12th anniversary today!
- mmmm earl grey tea
- Heading to Vancouver: [URL to map pinpointing current location]
- Happy birthday @GeorgeVeletsianos
- We are watching Star Wars The Empire Strikes Back tonight!

Stewart's (2015a) investigation of how networked scholarship lined up against Boyer's (1990) vision for scholarship determined that one of the key benefits for the participants in her study was that while networks enabled contribution on all of Boyer's components of scholarship, they also exceeded the boundaries of institutional academia. In other words, networked participation allowed scholars to be far more themselves, in their own estimations, than their institutional roles allow. For example, one participant in Stewart's (2015a, p. 55) study noted

> My role is a hybrid admin-academic role – as far as the university is considered I'm half and half but I consider myself an educator, so my networked participation is much more fulfilling, less limiting than my job title ... I couldn't live without that network because the way that I work and teach and learn is different from my immediate peers where I sit at the university – the level of exchange and challenge that I get on Twitter is really important to me.

This capacity of networks to allow scholars to round out their identities is rooted, in part, in the sharing of mundanities. Tweeting everyday activities allows people to connect to each other as people, and not just on professional topics. In a profession as hierarchical as academia, the ways in which networked conventions of casual everyday sharing allow for cross-status conversations is particularly interesting, and potentially valuable. A scholar in a related study (Stewart, 2015b, p.16) stated:

> I feel like Twitter is the Great Equalizer. Take a recent back and forth with the Dean of my college … I am too intimidated to talk to him and he has no idea who I am, and yet on Twitter he posted about being at Microsoft Research and I started asking him questions. He ended up tweeting pictures of things I was asking about etc., and we even traded a few jokes.

Scholars' participation in the "childhood walk" Internet meme also exemplifies the ways in which scholars' digital activities extend beyond scholarly matters. An Internet meme is a recognizable visual, verbal, aural or bodily enactment that spreads virally across the web by being slightly altered and then shared. Examples of popular memes include: LOLcats, Three Wolf Moon T-shirt, Numa Numa dance, the Harlem Shake videos, the Ice Bucket Challenge, and so on. "A childhood walk" was a concept developed by Internet performance artist Ze Frank, in which he asked individuals to use Google Maps – and in particular its Street View feature – to share stories and screenshots of childhood walks and memories. Numerous individuals contributed stories (archived at http://www.zefrank.com/the_walk/), and among those a number of researchers and educators shared their stories of childhood walks. These stories present a self that is often unseen in academic circles outside of conference gatherings and other small-group gatherings, and may enable individuals to develop relationships and bonds.

The public networked scholars observed in my investigations tend to share both professional and personal information. While the literature is largely premised on the argument that social media participation can enhance scholarly outcomes, this research highlights that the details that scholars share from their private lives also matter and contribute to overall social media experiences. Taken literally and out of context, scholars' microblogging updates may appear to have no real function, but seemingly unimportant tweets serve significant social purposes. Non-scholarly social interaction is "essential to forging bonds, affirming relationships, displaying bonds, and asserting and learning about hierarchies and alliances" (cf. Tufekci, 2008, p. 546), potentially leading to positive scholarly impacts. For example, learning that a colleague enjoys the same hobby as you do might be the tidbit of knowledge necessary to commence a conversation leading to future scholarly collaboration. On the other hand, however, knowledge gained from non-scholarly social interaction can alienate colleagues and hinder relationship-building when people have differing personal beliefs or vastly different boundaries around sharing.

Scholars' Hashtag Use: An Illustration of Scholars' Participation Online Extending Beyond Scholarship

By examining the hashtags that scholars use, we can gain insight into the degree to which scholarly participation online is focused on scholarly matters or whether it extends beyond those.

In examining the use of Twitter hashtags, Page (2012) shows that hashtags may fall into a number of categories. For example, hashtags are used to indicate fields of professional expertise and make professional identities visible and searchable (e.g., a scholar tagging his/her messages with #STEM, #ScienceEducation etc.), but are also used to contribute to national events such as politics and sports. In Veletsianos and Kimmons (2015), we found that popular hashtags used by education scholars related to three areas: education (e.g., #edchat, #highered, #edreform), civil rights or advocacy (e.g., #Ferguson, #BlackLivesMatter), and general Internet culture (e.g., #FF for Follow Friday, #TBT for Throwback Thursday). This result suggests that scholars' participation in and contributions to hashtags extends well beyond traditional notions of scholarship. While education hashtags are used to indicate professional expertise, scholars' online participation may also be understood to be influenced by temporal events that may or may not be scholarly in focus. For example, the marches and protests that originated in Ferguson, Missouri, in 2014 generated the hashtags #Ferguson and #BlackLivesMatter, which were prevalent in our study. Although some individuals within the sample we studied may have used the #Ferguson hashtag because it related to their area of expertise, the sheer volume of tweets pertaining to this topic and the number of individuals contributing to it suggests that at least some of those scholars may not have had a scholarly or professional connection to the topic.

The significance of this finding stems from the fact that nearly all frameworks devised to date to explain, explore, and augment scholarly practice (i.e., Social Scholarship, Digital Scholarship, Open Scholarship) focus on a narrow sliver of scholars' activities online, namely those that deal with scholarship, and ignore other fundamental aspects of online presence. Scholars however enact a wide range of activities online, and to understand scholars' online lives and participation researchers need to explore a wider range of activities. For instance, activities may be professional but not scholarly; discussing the impact of online learning on higher education may be a professional activity for all faculty but a scholarly activity only for those who study the topic. By examining scholars' digital activities without framing them as scholarly, we may be able to make sense of day-to-day facets of academic life such as the role of fun and humor in academics' online interactions, or the discourses used to describe academic life. The scholarly community lacks frameworks to investigate and understand the uniqueness and diversity of scholars' online and networked participation because online participation extends beyond scholarship, but current frameworks are incapable of accounting for this reality.

Networked Scholarship offers the breadth required to allow an examination of identity and experience beyond scholarly practice. While understanding *scholarly participation online* is significant, the research community would benefit from the further development and adoption of frameworks to understand *scholars' online participation* beyond scholarship. Future research in this area may seek to examine scholars' activism online (e.g., in relation to the adjunctification of higher education); scholars' online participation as it relates to civil rights issues like gender, sexual orientation, race, and violence; and scholars' lived experiences online.

Conclusion

The narratives of knowledge production/dissemination and public scholarship are pervasive in discussions pertaining to networked scholarship – so much so, that the higher education community tends to lose sight of the fact that networks are inherently human, and as such will be complicated and complex. Shifting our focus from *scholarly networks* to *scholars in networks* allows us to face the fact that scholars will engage, exist, and function within networks in a myriad of ways, and will perform both scholarly and non-scholarly activities in them.

12
CONCLUSION

The reality of scholars' experiences and participation on online networks is messy and complicated. So what? What are the implications of the findings presented in past chapters? What lessons can we draw moving forward? How should scholars and institutions of higher learning respond to the networked societies they find themselves in? Throughout the book, we explored the meaning, potential, and implications of networked scholarship. I've attempted to illuminate the complexity of the issues involved, and sought to balance the potential of networked scholarship with the tensions inherent in it, the state-of-the-art with what actually happens when scholars find themselves in networks.

The emergence of networked scholarship as a practice has extensive implications for scholars, scholarship, and academic institutions. What, then, are some broader conclusions that we can draw from this investigation?

The Scholar's Role

Networked scholarship is largely in a phase of ongoing development within the larger ever-fluctuating environment of higher education. Whether they recognize it or not, scholars are part of a complex techno-cultural system that is ever-changing in response to both internal and external stimuli, including technological innovations, political and economic climates, and dominant cultural values. Though such an understanding may lead to a certain level of trepidation regarding the shape of scholarship's uncertain future, scholars should take an active role in influencing and designing the future of scholarship in an increasingly networked and digital world.

Individual scholars and institutions, both networked and otherwise need to evaluate the purposes and functions of scholarship and take part in devising systems that reflect and safeguard these values of scholarly inquiry. A diverse range of scholars needs to be involved in making decisions regarding the systems of evaluation and promotion of networked scholarship in institutional settings. As with those in any community, early adopters (or in general, scholars who are engaging with or are embedded in networked scholarship) are susceptible to the risks of making decisions about the future of networked scholarship which may be arbitrary, prejudiced, or otherwise harmful to the community's well-being. Thus, scholars should be vigilant and reflective in their use of networked technologies as these continue to emerge and develop. Such vigilance should focus both on determining who profits from such practices and who is excluded from them so as to combat both under-use by some (e.g., those lacking entry to or knowledge of useful networks) and over-use or exploitation by those with the wealth, power, and prestige necessary to effectively strip mine sources (cf. Chander & Sunder, 2004). While solutions to these problems may not be simple, forward-thinking approaches to proactive prevention with regard to the protection of scholarly freedom, and the upholding of these early-adopted ideals, are superior to *post facto* reparation.

Doctoral Programs Should Teach Networked Scholarship

University curricula need to prepare future scholars to make sense of and productively participate in networked societies, especially because many of the practices and innovations inherent to networked scholarship appear to question traditional elements of scholarly practice and institutional norms (e.g., questioning peer-review, publishing work-in-progress, accessing literature through crowdsourcing). In other words, universities need to grapple with networked scholarship, as well as with the changing nature of scholarship, on a curricular level.

Networked scholarship curricula will need to balance a focus on *tools* and *issues*. The teaching of *tools* could instill future scholars with the abilities to use networked technologies productively. For instance, networked scholars might employ the services of text-mining techniques (e.g., Google Alerts) to track mentions of their name, areas of research, or publications such that they can keep track of and participate in discussions mentioning their work. Many trends, including the publication of journals in digital form, the pervasive use of institutional profiles, and the use of social media services for personal reasons combine to make it highly likely that scholars are already searchable and findable online. Thus, online presence is assumed to exist regardless of whether a scholar has taken any steps in cultivating such a presence, and the teaching of tools to manage one's presence may be necessary. The teaching of *issues* pertaining to networked scholarship is also significant. Scholars would benefit from making sense of issues such as networked societies, context collapse, alternative metrics, homophily, filter bubble, open access publishing, digital literacies, and community-engaged scholarship. For instance, doctoral preparation curricula might problematize the fact that while Twitter might allow researchers to follow one another and discuss topics of interest, such discussions may go unchallenged, if scholars are only followed by those who have similar educational training and beliefs to them. Further, future scholars will benefit greatly from gaining a well-rounded understanding of networks that does not privilege a technodeterministic perspective, but rather accounts for a sociocultural understanding of networks that positions them as places where knowledge is produced and disseminated, tensions and conflict are rampant, inequities exists, disclosures often occur, and identity is fragmented. University curricula might also prepare scholars to work in an increasingly uncertain world: what challenges will scholars face at their institutions or in the broader culture as they enact the practices described in this book?

The concept of "sharing" is a persistent finding in my research, and it might be a topic worth exploring in university curricula. The individuals who are embracing sharing practices are finding value in doing so, and often advocate that others should share too. It is not unusual for example to encounter quotes such as "good things happen to those who share," or "sharing is caring," or "education is sharing." These quotes illustrate and exemplify the values of the networked scholarship subculture. Faculty members have historically shared their work with each other (e.g., through letters, telephone calls, and conference presentations), but educators and researchers are increasingly sharing their scholarship online in open spaces as well. Wiley and Green (2012, p. 82) even argue that "[e]ducation is, first and foremost, an enterprise of sharing. In fact, sharing is the sole means by which education is effected." However, education – both K–12 and higher education – has generally lacked a culture of sharing. Barab, Makinster, Moore, and Cunningham (2001) note that "change efforts [in K–12] have often been unsuccessful due in large part to the lack of a culture of sharing among teachers (Chism, 1985)." A core value of this subculture seems to be that *sharing should be treated as a scholarly practice*. As such, future scholars may benefit from an examination, and critique, of this practice to understand both its implications as well as its ideologies. Significantly, doctoral preparation curricula may need to grapple with how "sharing" interfaces with "open practice" and what the implications of various means of sharing are for scholars and the academy. For example, posting copyrighted scholarship on Academia.edu may constitute a form of sharing, but this is not the same as "openness." Academia.edu provides a distribution mechanism in the form of a social network, but does little to foster and promote open licensing and Creative Commons policies with respect to scholarship.

A Parallel Scholarly Environment is Arising – and Institutions/ Scholars need to Understand it

Siemens (2013) argued that a shadow education system has been developing, one in which individuals use the Internet to learn without the support of educational institutions. He argues that this has occurred as a result of institutions of learning having failed to recognize the demand for the unique needs of complex contemporary societies. While this argument focuses on learners, a similar situation is occurring in terms of scholarly practice: the shadow education system that Siemens sees arising encompasses a scholarly academy that runs parallel to the traditional one. This environment, facilitated and encouraged by online social networks, serves scholarly functions and features and supports the development, sharing, negotiation, and evaluation of knowledge. In this parallel environment, scholars have,

- supported peers and students regardless of hierarchy and institutional affiliation;
- provided advice and care in time of need;
- commented on peers' in-progress manuscripts;
- delivered guest lectures or taught open courses; and
- created and shared videos and other media summarizing their scholarship.

Many of these activities have occurred with little or no institutional support and in many instances with little or no institutional oversight. My conversations with many scholars lead me to believe that the general feeling is that many of these valued activities would not have occurred had institutions been more involved. While such a critique of the institution is damning, the feeling is often expressed in a somber way, in a way that demonstrates scholars' desires for institutions to support these endeavours. After all, many scholars find them to be worthwhile.

This is not to say that the emerging parallel scholarly environment is always effective and fair. Many of the power relations and inequities that exist in the traditional scholarly environment are reproduced in networks, and even though signals of influence and impact may differ, they may still be incapable of escaping reductionist agendas of quantification (e.g., social media metrics replace citation and journal metrics).

Institutions will have to consider how the concept of academic freedom aligns with the activities of networked scholars. At a very basic level institutions will have to grapple with the drafting of appropriate social media policies, especially as the values of "openness" and "transparency" that are often imbued in this emerging scholarly environment appear to be in conflict with prevailing policies governing faculty members' social media use. As reported by Lough and Samek (2014), the current trend in social software policies in the Canadian post-secondary sector is to control and manage social media participation – to inspect and police digital activity. This trend is not limited to Canada of course, as illustrated by the description of the Kansas Board of Regents social media policy described in chapter 6. While social media policies need to support a variety of needs, they also need to recognize the increasingly integral role digital participation plays in scholars' lives, the complexity of online social networks as places where teaching, learning, and research occur, the role of social media as places where the personal and the professional intersect, and the fact that social media platforms often serve as places of debate and spirited exchange of ideas. At the very least, institutions should clarify their stance on whether academic freedom extends to social media speech. Such a stance should be taken *ex ante*, and not *ex post facto*. Other scholars have recently supported this perspective. For instance, Daniels (2015) noted that institutions should "reimagine a wider definition of academic freedom as explicitly tied to the faculty member who may communicate in a variety of ways, including digitally mediated ones" and argued that "it is possible to simultaneously expand academic freedom in a digitally networked era *and* stand for values that reject racism" (emphasis mine). Further, fruitfully, Murphy (2014, p. 228) argued that institutions should introduce "protective social media policies that explicitly recognize the application of academic freedom to the social media context." How these perspectives interact with local laws is a matter that needs further analysis beyond the scope of this conclusion, though in writing about the Salaita affair, LeRoy (2015, pp. 164–166), a law scholar in the United States offers a hint of clarity when he notes that past law cases may suggest that "tweets that disrupt a school's mission or operations are not protected by the First Amendment" including when "a university makes a reasonable prediction that students or faculty would feel intimidated by personally abusive or demeaning speech."

One significant reason for which institutions and scholars need to understand the parallel scholarly system that is arising is because it might increasingly come to be used in decisions that impact the ways that higher education institutions operate. With increasing calls to develop alternative metrics to evaluate scholarly work, scholars and institutions might turn to social media metrics as indicators of impact and reach. While social media metrics may be worthwhile indicators to examine in a broad portfolio of quantitative and qualitative evidence of scholarly work, care should be taken to recognize that such metrics may suffer from problems similar to those that traditional indicators of scholarly work suffer from. In the same way that citation counts do not necessarily indicate excellence, Twitter follower counts or paper download counts might not necessarily imply positive impact or outreach.

Promotion and Tenure/Permanency Policies need to Recognize and Foster Networked Scholarship

Having noted the need to be critical of the metrics arising from networked participation, it should be noted that it behooves higher education institutions to develop broader conceptions of what constitutes scholarship. Is a piece of software scholarship? Is a blog post scholarship? Is networked participation scholarship? Which aspects of networked participation are scholarship and how would an institution evaluate their legitimacy? If processes are being developed to evaluate not just the production, but also the rigour and impact of traditional scholarly artifacts, what processes need to be developed to evaluate scholarly activity that does not fit neatly into definitions of scholarship created in a pre-networked era? These questions point to the further development of promotion and tenure policies (or permanency criteria) such that they recognize and foster networked scholarship, legitimizing it within the academy not only as public scholarship, but as part of what enriches and broadens knowledge within the academy.

However, attempting to widen the circle of networked participation risks both having it reduced to altmetrics, which only extends the hyper-rationalized logic of impact that already dominates the journal publishing system, or opening the academy further to the logics of commercialism and media attention that dominates networks. As modern universities are operating within a world increasingly dominated by managerial and corporate practices that favour quantitative metrics, scholars' digital participation may at times stand in stark contrast to and defy such evaluation metrics. Defining networked scholarship in terms of metrics for evaluation purposes may be an efficient route, but it will ultimately be ineffective.

Research Should Focus on Issues, not Technologies

Future research on networked scholarship should focus on particular issues pertaining to the topic – not on technology. Rather than posing questions about Facebook, Twitter, YouTube, and any other technology available at the time that you are reading this book, researchers should be posing questions about scholarly identity, impact, influence, relationships, challenges, successes, and tensions. Technologies change rapidly, and any research focusing on the particulars of the technology will quickly become obsolete.

Tensions and Conflicts

As we have seen, tensions and conflicts are pervasive in networked scholarship. Evangelizing networked, digital, social, and open scholarship without acknowledging the existence of tensions is detrimental to the field and misleading to the scholars who may be considering becoming more networked, more open, and more "digital." By now, you should have a greater understanding of the tensions and conflicts in emergent forms of scholarship. Thus, I hope that if a peer, and especially a junior colleague, asks for your input on the topic, you will be able to provide a nuanced discussion of both the potential and the limitations of networked scholarship. Such nuanced discussion might include consideration of the following three issues:

- What counts as influence in academia? Sometimes networks enable junior scholars to become known and recognized for the work they do at an international scale, but not in their institutions. Thus, networks pose implicit challenges to academic hierarchy, creating odd identity spaces.

- What counts as public speech? The Steven Salaita affair brought to the forefront debates pertaining to freedom of speech and academic freedom, and the terrain is both volatile and opaque.
- How do networks intersect with contingent employment in higher education institutions? While the expectation of constant presence and availability through networks impacts many scholars, the reality is that junior and contingent scholars' lives will be the ones that will be inundated, often with no recompense, by the expectation that they be "always on."

In Closing

Emergent forms of scholarship have the potential to enhance scholarly endeavours. But to do so, institutions and scholars may need to pursue paradigmatic shifts in the ways that they think about education, knowledge, learning, teaching, and research. Networked scholarship also requires shifts in the ways that we view our identity as scholars, in the ways we think about media, and in the ways that we think about social stratification. In the process of creating scholarly and educational systems for the future, we, as a scholarly community, need to remain critical of the systems we are creating and question our assumptions and practices. While such systems might arise from the inadequacies and shortcomings of the status quo, this does not make them exemplary or just.

REFERENCES

Ajjan, H. & Hartshorne, R. (2008). Investigating faculty decisions to adopt Web 2.0 technologies: Theory and empirical tests. *The Internet & Higher Education, 11*(2), 71–80.

Åkerlind, G. S. (2005). Postdoctoral researchers: Roles, functions and career prospects. *Higher Education Research & Development, 24*(1), 21–40.

Alexa Top 500 Global Sites. (2015). Retrieved June 1, 2015 from http://www.alexa.com/topsites

Alexander, K. (2007). Balancing the challenges of today with the promise of tomorrow: A presidential perspective. In D'Ambrosio, M., & Ehrenberg, R. (Eds.), *Transformational change in higher education: positioning colleges and universities for future success* (pp. 16–29). Cheltenham, UK: Edward Elgar.

Amado, M., Ashton, K., Ashton, S., Bostwick, J., Clements, G., Darnall, R., Drysdale, J., Francis, J., Harrison, B., Nan, V., Nisse, A., Preston, J., Randall, D., Rino, J., Robinson, J., Snyder, A., & Wiley, D. (2011). *Project Management for Instructional Designers*. Retrieved August 13, 2015 from http://pm4id.org/

Andersen, D. (2003). *Digital scholarship in the tenure, promotion, and review process*. New York, NY: M. E. Sharpe.

Anonymous. (2014, May 22.) Unsolicited article review [Web log post]. Retrieved May 27, 2015 from http://academickindness.tumblr.com/post/86499668061/unsolicited-article-review

Aro, M. & Olkinuora, E. (2007). Riding the information highway – towards a new kind of learning. *International Journal of Lifelong Education, 26*(4), 385–398.

Ayers, E. (2004, January 30). Doing scholarship on the web: 10 years of triumphs and a disappointment. *The Chronicle of Higher Education*. Retrieved June 1, 2015 from http://chronicle.com/article/Doing-Scholarship-on-the-Web-/18713

Baker, D. (2008). From needles and haystacks to elephants and fleas: Strategic information management in the information age. *New Review of Academic Librarianship, 14*(1/2), 1–16.

Barab, S., Makinster, J., Moore, J., & Cunningham, D. (2001). Designing and building an on-line community: The struggle to support sociability in the inquiry learning forum. *Educational Technology Research and Development, 49*(4), 71–96.

Batson, C. D., Ahmad, N., & Tsang, J. A. (2002). Four motives for community involvement. *Journal of Social Issues, 58*(3), 429–445.

Bauder, H. (2006). The segmentation of academic labour: A Canadian example. *ACME: An International E-Journal for Critical Geographies, 4*(2), 228–239.

Bergland, C. (2014). The "Ivory Tower" appears reluctant to use social media. *Psychology Today.* Retrieved April 12, 2014 from https://www.psychologytoday.com/blog/the-athletes-way/201403/the-ivory-tower-appears-reluctant-use-social-media [Based on Michigan State Press Release: http://msutoday.msu.edu/news/2014/ivory-tower-bucking-social-media/]

Binkley, R. C. (1935). New tools for men of letters. *The Yale Review, 24,* 519–537.

Björk, B.-C., Welling, P., Laakso, M., Majlender, P., Hedlund, T., & Guðni, G. (2010). Open access to the scientific journal literature: Situation 2009. *PLoS ONE, 5*(6): e11273.

Blyth, E., Shardlow, S. M., Masson, H., Lyons, K., Shaw, I., & White, S. (2010). Measuring the quality of peer-reviewed publications in social work: Impact factors—liberation or liability? *Social Work Education, 29*(2), 120–136.

Bonk, C. J. (2009). *The world is open: How Web technology is revolutionizing education.* San Francisco, CA: John Wiley & Sons.

Borgman, C. (2007). *Scholarship in the digital age: Information, infrastructure, and the Internet.* Hong Kong: MIT Press.

Borup, J., Graham, C. R., & Velasquez, A. (2013). Technology-mediated caring: Building relationships between students and instructors in online K-12 learning environments. In M. Newberry, A. Gallant, & P. Riley (Eds.), *Advances in research on teaching: Vol. 18. Emotions in school: Understanding how the hidden curriculum influences relationships, leadership, teaching, and learning* (pp. 183–202). Bingley, UK: Emerald Books.

Boshier, R. (2009). Why is the scholarship of teaching and learning such a hard sell? *Higher Education Research & Development, 28*(1), 1–15.

Bowman, T. D. (2015). Differences in personal and professional tweets of scholars. *Aslib Journal of Information Management, 67*(3), 356–371.

boyd, d. (2008). Facebook's privacy trainwreck: Exposure, invasion, and social convergence. *Convergence, 14*(1), 13–20.

boyd, d. (2009). Streams of content, limited attention: The flow of information through social media. *Web2.0 Expo* [Conference]. New York, NY. November 17.

boyd, d. (2011). Social network sites as networked publics: Affordances, dynamics, and implications. In Z. Papcharissi (Ed.), *A networked self* (pp. 39–58). New York, NY: Routledge.

boyd, d. (2014). Am I a Blogger? Talk given at BlogHer '14 [Conference]. San Jose, CA. July 24-26. Transcript retrieved February 11, 2015 from http://www.zephoria.org/thoughts/archives/2014/09/15/am-i-a-blogger.html

boyd, d. (2015). Social media: A phenomenon to be analyzed. *Social Media + Society, 1*(1), 1–2. doi: 10.1177/2056305115580148

Boyer, E. (1990). *Scholarship reconsidered: Priorities for the professoriate.* Princeton, NJ: The Carnegie Foundation for the Advancement of Teaching.

Briggle, A. & Mitcham, C. (2009). Embedding and networking: Conceptualizing experience in a technosociety. *Technology in Society, 31*(4), 374–383.

Brown, R. A. (2015, May 12). Letter from President Brown. Retrieved June 1, 2015 from http://www.bu.edu/president/letters-writings/letters/2015/5-12/

Browser Statistics. (2015). Web Statistics and Trends. Retrieved July 1, 2015 from http://www.w3schools.com/browsers/browsers_stats.asp

Buckley, S. & Du Toit, A. (2010). Academics leave your ivory tower: Form communities of practice. *Educational Studies, 36*(5), 493–503.

Budapest Open Access Initiative. (2002). Retrieved July 30, 2010 from http://www.soros.org/openaccess/read.shtml

Bull, G., Thompson, A., Searson, M., Garofalo, J., Park, J., Young, C., & Lee, J. (2008). Connecting informal and formal learning experiences in the age of participatory media. *Contemporary Issues in Technology and Teacher Education, 8*(2), 100–107.

Burrows, R. (2012). Living with the h-index? Metric assemblages in the contemporary academy. *The Sociological Review, 60*(2), 355–372.

Burton, G. (2009). The open scholar [Web log post]. Academic Evolution. Retrieved August 12, 2010 from http://www.academicevolution.com/2009/08/the-open-scholar.html

Casadevall, A. & Fang, F. C. (2009). Is peer review censorship? *Infection and Immunity, 77*(4), 1273–1274.

Chander, A. & Sunder, M. (2004). The romance of the public domain. *California Law Review, 92*(5), 1331–1373.

Charfauros, K. H. & Tierney, W. G. (1999). Part-time faculty in colleges and universities: trends and challenges in a turbulent environment. *Journal of Personnel Evaluation in Education, 13*(2), 141–151.

Chism, N. (1985). The place of peer interaction in teacher development: Findings from a case study. Paper presented at the 1985 Annual Meeting of the American Educational Research Association (AERA), Chicago, IL.

Christensen, C. M., Horn, M. B., & Johnson, C. W. (2008). *Disrupting class: How disruptive innovation will change the way the world learns.* New York, NY: McGraw-Hill.

Clawson, D. (2009). Tenure and the future of the university. *Science, 324*, 1147–1148.

Coalition on the Academic Workforce. (2012). *A portrait of part-time faculty members.* Retrieved August 13, 2015 from http://www.academicworkforce.org/CAW_portrait_2012.pdf

Coddington R. (2010) Professors' Use of Technology in Teaching. The Chronicle of Higher Education. Retrieved on June 2, 2015 from http://chronicle.com/article/article-content/123682

Cohen, L. (2007). Social scholarship on the rise [Web log post]. Library 2.0: An Academic's Perspective. Retrieved August 12, 2010 from http://liblogs.albany.edu/library20/2007/04/social_scholarship_on_the_rise.html

Cohen, P. (2010). Scholars test web alternative to peer review. *The New York Times.* Retrieved September 12, 2010 from http://www.nytimes.com/2010/08/24/arts/24peer.html?pagewanted=2

Cole, S., Cole, J., & Simon, G. (1981). Chance and consensus in peer review. *Science, 214*, 881–886.

Colson, D. (2014). On the ground in Kansas: Social media, academic freedom, and the fight for higher education. Retrieved May 11, 2015 from http://www.aaup.org/file/Colson.pdf

Confused on the Tenure Track. (2015). Let's talk about Twitter. Retrieved May 23, 2015 from https://www.insidehighered.com/advice/2015/05/20/essay-issues-facing-young-academics-social-media

Connaway, S., Lanclos, D., & Hood, E. (2013). "I always stick with the first thing that comes up on Google..." Where People Go for Information, What They Use, and Why. EDUCAUSE Review Online. Retrieved August 12, 2015 from http://www.educause.edu/ero/article/i-always-stick-first-thing-comes-google-where-people-go-information-what-they-use-and-why

Coiro, J., Knobel, M., Lankshear, C., & Leu, D. (2008). Central issues in new literacies and new literacies research. In J. Coiro, M. Knobel, C, Lankshear, C., & D. Leu (Eds.), *Handbook of research on new literacies* (p. 1–21). New York: Lawrence Erlbaum.

Correia, A. (2012). Breaking the mold: an educational perspective on diffusion of innovation. Retrieved October 21, 2015 from http://en.wikibooks.org/wiki/Breaking_the_Mold:_An_Educational_Perspective_on_Diffusion_of_Innovation

Costa, C. (2014). Outcasts on the inside: Academics reinventing themselves online. *International Journal of Lifelong Education, 34*(2), 194–210.

Cottom, T. M. (2015a). "Who do you think you are?": When marginality meets academic microcelebrity. *Ada: A Journal of Gender, New Media, and Technology.* Retrieved May 19, 2015 from http://adanewmedia.org/2015/04/issue7-mcmillancottom/

Cottom, T. M. (2015b). Credit scores, life chances, and algorithms. Retrieved August 13, 2015 from http://tressiemc.com/2015/05/30/credit-scores-life-chances-and-algorithms/?utm_content=buffer26ed4&utm_medium=social&utm_source=twitter.com&utm_campaign=buffer

Couros, A. (2009). Visualizing open/networked teaching. Retrieved June 1, 2015 from http://educationaltechnology.ca/couros/1335

Couros, A. (2013). My dad [Web log post]. Retrieved May 29, 2015 from http://educationaltechnology.ca/couros/2321

Crawford, L (2014). Introducing Academic Breakfast [Web log post]. Retrieved May 12, 2015 from http://academic-breakfast.tumblr.com/post/86291254333/introducing-academic-breakfast

Crenshaw, K. (1989). Demarginalizing the intersection of race and sex: A black feminist critique of antidiscrimination doctrine, feminist theory, and antiracist politics. *The University of Chicago Legal Forum, 140*, 139–167.

Cuban, L. (2001). *Oversold and underused: Reforming schools through technology 1980–2000.* Cambridge, MA: Harvard University Press.

Daniels, J. (2015). Twitter, knowledge creation and academic freedom in a digital era. Manuscript submitted for publication. Retrieved June 20, 2015 from https://www.academia.edu/11458656/Twitter_Knowledge_Creation_and_Academic_Freedom_in_a_Digital_Era

Dayter, D. (2014). Self-praise in micro-blogging. *Journal of Pragmatics, 61*, 91–102.

De Groote, S. L. & Dorsch, J. L. (2001). Online journals: impact on print journal usage. *Bulletin of the Medical Library Association, 89*(4), 372–378.

Delen, D. & Al-Hawamdeh, S. (2009). A holistic framework for knowledge discovery and management. *Communications of the ACM, 52*(6), 141–145.

DesGarennes, C. (2014, September 2). Salaita prompted donors' fury. The News-Gazette. Retrieved July 20, 2015 from http://www.news-gazette.com/news/local/2014-09-02/salaita-prompted-donors-fury.html

Donath, J. & boyd, d. (2004). Public displays of connection. *BT Technology Journal, 22*(4), 71–82.

Dorf, M. C. (2014). Academic freedom in the Salaita case. Verdict. Retrieved June 1, 2014 from https://verdict.justia.com/2014/08/13/academic-freedom-salaita-case

Dron, J. & Anderson, T. (2009). How the crowd can teach. In S. Hatzipanagos & S. Warburton (Eds.), *Handbook of research on social software and developing ontologies* (pp. 1–17). London: IGI Global.

Ehrenberg, R. G. (2000). *Tuition rising.* Cambridge, MA: Harvard University Press.

Elsevier. (2012). Get found—optimize your research articles for search engines. Retrieved June 1, 2015 from http://www.elsevier.com/connect/get-found-optimize-your-research-articles-for-search-engines

Eysenbach, G. (2006). Citation advantage of open access articles. *PLoS Biol, 4*(5): e157.

Fang, F. C., Steen, R. G., & Casadevall, A. (2012). Misconduct accounts for the majority of retracted scientific publications. *Proceedings of the National Academy of Sciences, 109*(42), 17028–17033.

Flaherty, C. (2014). "In a hurricane." *Inside Higher Ed.* Retrieved June 1, 2015 from https://www.insidehighered.com/news/2014/08/15/cary-nelson-faces-backlash-over-his-views-controversial-scholar

Ford, K., Veletsianos, G., & Resta, P. (2014). The structure and characteristics of #PhDChat, an emergent online social network. *Journal of Interactive Media in Education.* Retrieved April 11, 2014 from http://jime.open.ac.uk/jime/article/view/2014-08

Foster, K., Bergin, K., Mckenna, A., Millard, D., Perez, L., Prival, J., Rainey, D., Sevian, H., VanderPutten, E., & Hamos, J. (2010). Partnerships for STEM education. *Science, 329,* 906–907.

Friedman, T. L. (2005). *The world is flat: A brief history of the twenty-first century.* New York: Farrar, Straus, and Giroux.

Furlough, M. (2010). Open access, education research, and discovery. *The Teachers College Record, 112*(10), 2623–2648.

Garnet, F. & Ecclesfield, N. (2011). Towards a framework for cocreating open scholarship. *Proceedings of the Association for Learning Technologies Conference (ALTC).*

Gašević, D., Dawson, S., & Siemens, G. (2015). Let's not forget: Learning analytics are about learning. *TechTrends, 59*(1), 64–71.

Gee, J. (2009). Identity without identification. In A. Carter, T. Lillis, & S. Parkin (Eds.), *Why writing matters: Issues of access and identity in writing research and pedagogy* (pp. 45–46). Philadelphia, PA: John Benjamins Publishing Company.

Goffman, E. (1959) *The presentation of self in everyday life.* New York: Anchor.

Goodyear, R. K., Brewer, D. J., Gallagher, K. S., Tracey, T. J., Claiborn, C. D., Lichtenberg, J. W., & Wampold, B. (2009). The intellectual foundations of education: Core journals and their impacts on scholarship and practice. *Educational Researcher, 38*(9), 700–706.

Gowers, T. & Nielsen, M. (2009). Massively collaborative mathematics. *Nature, 461*(7266), 879–81.

Greenhow, C. (2009). Social scholarship: Applying social networking technologies to research practices. *Knowledge Quest, 37*(4), 42–47.

Greenhow, C. & Gleason, B. (2014). Social scholarship: Reconsidering scholarly practices in the age of social media. *British Journal of Educational Technology, 45*(3), 392–402.

Greenhow, C., Robelia, B., & Hughes, J. (2009). Learning, teaching, and scholarship in a digital age: Web 2.0 and classroom research: What path should we take now? *Educational Researcher, 38*(4), 233–259.

Griffin, M. (n.d.). Unexpected email [Web log post]. Retrieved May 27, 2015 from http://academickindness.tumblr.com/post/78316504614/unexpected-email

Gruzd, A., Wellman, B., & Takhteyev, Y. (2011). Imagining Twitter as an imagined community. *American Behavioural Scientist, 55*(10), 1294–1318.

Hajjem, C., Harnad, S., & Gingras, Y. (2005) Ten-year cross-disciplinary comparison of the growth of open access and how it increases research citation impact. *IEEE Data Engineering Bulletin, 28*(4), 39–47.

Hall, R. (2011). Revealing the transformatory moment of learning technology: The place of critical social theory. *Research in Learning Technology, 19*(3), 273–284.

Harnad, S. (2008). Waking OA's "Slumbering Giant": The university's mandate to mandate open access. *New Review of Information Networking, 14*(1), 51–68.

Heap, T. & Minocha, S. (2012). An empirically grounded framework to guide blogging for digital scholarship. *Research In Learning Technology, 20.* doi:10.3402/rlt.v20i0.19195

Hermida, A. (2015). Power plays on social media. *Social Media + Society, 1*(1), 1–2.

Hilton, J. & Wiley, D. (2010). Free: Why authors are giving books away on the Internet. *Tech Trends, 54*(2), 43–49.

Hilton, J., Graham, C., Rich, P., & Wiley, D. (2010). Using online technologies to extend a classroom to learners at a distance. *Distance Education, 31*(1), 77–92.

Ho, A. D., Reich, J., Nesterko, S. O., Seaton, D. T., Mullaney, T., Waldo, J., & Chuang, I. (2014). HarvardX and MITx: The first year of open online courses, Fall 2012–Summer 2013. Available at SSRN: http://ssrn.com/abstract=2381263 or http://dx.doi.org/10.2139/ssrn.2381263

Hough, M. G. (2009). Keeping it to ourselves: Technology, privacy, and the loss of reserve. *Technology in Society, 31*(4), 406–413.

Hughes, J., Thomas, R. & Scharber, C. (2006). Assessing technology integration: The RAT–replacement, amplification, and transformation framework. In C. Crawford (Ed.), *Proceedings of Society for Information Technology & Teacher Education International Conference 2006* (pp. 1616–1620). Chesapeake, VA: AACE.

Hurt, C. & Yin, T. (2006). Blogging while untenured and other extreme sports. *Berkman Center for Internet & Society.* Retrieved August 13, 2015 from http://papers.ssrn.com/sol3/papers.cfm?abstract_id=898046

Hutchings, P. & Shulman, L. (1999). The scholarship of teaching: New elaborations, new developments. *Change, 31*(5), 10–15.

Ivanič, R. (1998). *Writing and identity: The discoursal construction of identity in academic writing.* Philadelphia, PA: John Benjamins Publishing Company.

Jaschik, S. (2014, August 6). Out of a job. *Inside Higher Ed.* Retrieved August 13, 2015 fromhttps://www.insidehighered.com/news/2014/08/06/u-illinois-apparently-revokes-job-offer-controversial-scholar#ixzz39gASNRzT

Jenkins, H., Clinton K., Purushotma, R., Robinson, A. J., & Weigel, M. (2006). *Confronting the challenges of participatory culture: Media education for the 21st century.* Chicago, IL: The MacArthur Foundation.

Jenkins, H., Purushotma, R., Weigel, M., Clinton K., & Robinson, A.J. (2009). *Confronting the challenges of participatory culture: Media education for the 21st century.* Cambridge, MA: The MIT Press.

Jenkins, J. (2006). Constructivism. In F. W. English (Ed.), *Encyclopedia of Educational Leadership and Administration* (pp. 195–199). Thousand Oaks, CA: Sage Reference.

Jenkins, R. (2014, February 17). We have to protect ourselves. *The Chronicle of Higher Education.* Retrieved August 13, 2015 from https://chronicle.com/article/We-Have-to-Protect-Ourselves/144775

Katz, R. (2010). Scholars, scholarship, and the scholarly enterprise in the digital age. *Educause Review, 45*(2), 44–56.

Keashly, L. & Neuman, J.H. (2010). Faculty experiences with bullying in higher education: Causes, consequences, and management. *Administrative Theory & Praxis, 32*(1), 48–70.

Kiernan, V. (2000). Rewards remain dim for professors who pursue digital scholarship. *The Chronicle of Higher Education.* Retrieved August 10, 2010 from http://chronicle.com/article/Rewards-Remain-Dim-for/6441

Kieslinger, B. (2015). Academic peer pressure in social media: Experiences from the heavy, the targeted and the restricted user. *First Monday, 20*(6). doi:10.5210/fm.v20i6.5854

Kimmons, R. (2014). Emergent forms of technology-influenced scholarship. In M. Khosrow-Pour (Ed.), *Encyclopedia of Information Science and Technology*, 3rd ed. (pp. 2481–2488). IGI Global.

Kimmons, R. & Veletsianos, G. (2014). The Fragmented Educator 2.0: Social networking sites, acceptable identity fragments, and the identity constellation. *Computers & Education, 72*, 292–301.

King, K. (2002). Educational technology professional development as transformative learning opportunities. *Computers & Education, 39*(3), 283–297.

Kirkup, G. (2010). Academic blogging: Academic practice and academic identity. *London Review of Education, 8*(1), 75–84.

Kjellberg, S. (2010). I am a blogging researcher: Motivations for blogging in a scholarly context. *First Monday, 15*(8).

Kop, R. & Hill, A. (2008). Connectivism: Learning theory of the future or vestige of the past? *International Review of Research in Open and Distance Learning, 9*(3), 1–13.

Kumashiro, K., Pinar, W., Graue, E., Grant, C., Benham, M., Heck, R., Scheurich, J., Luke, A., & Luke, C. (2005). Thinking collaboratively about the peer-review process for journal-article publication. *Harvard Educational Review, 75*(3), 257–285.

Lane, L. (2009). Insidious pedagogy: How course management systems impact teaching. *First Monday, 14*(10).

Latour, B. (2004). Why has critique run out of steam? From matters of fact to matters of concern. *Critical Inquiry, 30*(2), 225–248.

Lave, J. & Wenger, E. (1991). *Situated learning: Legitimate peripheral participation.* New York: Cambridge University Press.

Lee, R. K. (1997). Romantic and electronic stalking in a college context. *William & Mary Journal of Women and the Law, 4*, 373–465. Retrieved April 1, 2015 from http:// scholarship.law.wm.edu/cgi/viewcontent.cgi?article=1263&context=wmjowl

Lemke, J. & Van Helden, C. (2009). New learning cultures: Identities, media, and networks. In R. Goodfellow, & M. Lamy (Eds.), *Learning Cultures in Online Education* (pp. 151–169). New York, NY: Continuum International Publishing Group.

Leonard, D. (2012). The inked academic body. *The Chronicle of Higher Education.* Retrieved October 26, 2012 from http://chronicle.com/blogs/conversation/2012/10/25/ the-inked-academic-body/

LeRoy, M. H. (2015). #AcademicFreedom: Twitter and first amendment rights for professors. *Notre Dame Law Review Online, 90*, 158–167.

Lough, T. & Samek, T. (2014). Canadian university social software guidelines and academic freedom: An alarming labour trend. *The Digital Future of Education, 21*, 45–56.

Lowenthal, P. & Dunlap, J. (2012). Intentional Web presence: 10 SEO strategies every academic needs to know. *Educause Review Online.* Retrieved June 1, 2015 from http://www.educause.edu/ero/article/intentional-web-presence-10-seo-strategies-every-academic-needs-know

Lowenthal, P. & Muth, R. (2009). Constructivism. In E. F. Provenzo (Ed.), *Encyclopedia of the Social and Cultural Foundations of Education* (pp. 177–179). Thousand Oaks, CA: Sage Publications Inc.

Lupton, D. A. (2014). *"Feeling Better Connected": Academics' use of social media.* Canberra: News & Media Research Centre, University of Canberra. Retrieved August 13, 2015 from http://www.canberra.edu.au/faculties/arts-design/attachments/pdf/n-and-mrc/ Feeling-Better-Connected-report-final.pdf

MacFarlane, B. (2011). The morphing of academic practice: Unbundling and the rise of the para-academic. *Higher Education Quarterly, 65*(1), 59–73.

Malesky, L. A. & Peters, C. (2012). Defining appropriate professional behavior for faculty and university students on social networking websites. *Higher Education, 63*(1), 135–151.

Mewburn, I. & Thomson, P. (2013) Why do academics blog? An analysis of audiences, purposes and challenges. *Studies in Higher Education, 38*(8), 1105–1119.

Moran, M., Seaman, J., & Tinti-Kane, H. (2011). Teaching, learning, and sharing: How today's higher education faculty use social media for work and for play [Web log post]. Pearson Learning Solutions. Retrieved September 10, 2011 from http://files.eric.ed.gov/fulltext/ED535130.pdf

Moran, M. & Tinti-Kane, H. (2013). Social media for teaching and learning [Web log post]. Pearson Learning Solutions. Retrieved June 1, 2015 from http://www.pearsonlearningsolutions.com/assets/downloads/reports/social-media-for-teaching-and-learning-2013-report.pdf

Morrison, J. (2003). U.S. higher education in transition. *On the Horizon, 11*(1), 6–10.

Murphy, M. H. (2014). The views expressed represent mine alone: Academic freedom and social media. *SCRIPT-ed, 11*(3), 210–228.

Nardi, B. A., Schiano, D. J., & Gumbrecht, M. (2004). Blogging as social activity, or, would you let 900 million people read your diary? *Proceedings of the 2004 ACM Conference on Computer Supported Cooperative Work* (pp. 222–231).

Nature (2006). Peer review and fraud. *Nature, 444*, 971–972.

Neylon, C., & Wu, S. (2009). Article-level metrics and the evolution of scientific impact. *PLoS Biology, 7*(11), e1000242.

Nielsen, M. (2012). *Reinventing discovery: The new era of networked science.* Princeton, NJ: Princeton University Press.

Nissani, M. (1997). Ten cheers for interdisciplinarity: The case for interdisciplinary knowledge and research. *The Social Science Journal, 34*(2), 201–216.

Oblinger, D. G. (2010). From the campus to the future. *EDUCAUSE Review, 45*(1), 42–52.

Owens, S. (2014). How Reddit created the world's largest dialogue between scientists and the general public [Web log post]. Retrieved January 7, 2015 from http://www.simonowens.net/how-reddit-created-the-worlds-largest-dialogue-between-scientists-and-the-general-public

Page, R. (2012). The linguistics of self-branding and micro-celebrity in Twitter: The role of hashtags. *Discourse & Communication, 6*(2), 181–201.

Palmer, C., Teffeau, L., & Pirmann, C., (2009). *Scholarly information practices in the online environment: Themes from the literature and implications for library service development.* Report commissioned by OCLC Research. Retrieved April 18, 2011 from http://www.oclc.org/programs/publications/reports/2009-02.pdf

Papert, S. (1987). Computer criticism vs. technocentric thinking. *Educational Researcher, 16*(1), 22–30.

Pariser, E. (2011). *The filter bubble: What the Internet is hiding from you.* London: Viking/Penguin Press.

Pearce, N., Weller, M., Scanlon, E., & Kinsley, S. (2010). Digital scholarship considered: How new technologies could transform academic work in education. *In Education: Exploring our Connective Educational Landscape, 16*(1), 33–44.

Pellino, G., Blackburn, R., & Boberg, A. (1984). The dimensions of academic scholarship: Faculty and administrator views. *Research in Higher Education, 20*(1), 103–115.

Perkins, R. & Lowenthal, P. (2015). *Open access journals in educational technology: Results of a survey of experienced users.* Manuscript submitted for publication.

Peter, S., & Deimann, M. (2013). On the role of openness in education: A historical reconstruction. *Open Praxis, 5*(1), 7–14.

Pinar, W. (2005). On the politics of professional practice. *Harvard Educational Review, 75*(3), 266–268.

Popovich, N. G. & Abel, S. R. (2002). The need for a broadened definition of faculty scholarship and creativity. *American Journal of Pharmaceutical Education, 66*(1), 59–65.

Priem, J. & Hemminger, B. H. (2010). Scientometrics 2.0: New metrics of scholarly impact on the social web. *First Monday, 15*(7).

Priem, J., Taraborelli, D., Groth, P., & Neylon, C. (2010). Altmetrics: A manifesto. Retrieved August 13, 2015 from http://altmetrics.org/manifesto/

Public Library of Science (2010). *Article level metrics.* Retrieved September 14, 2010 from http://article-level-metrics.plos.org/

Purdy, J. & Walker, J. (2010). Valuing digital scholarship: Exploring the changing realities of intellectual work. *Profession, 19*, 177–195.

Raymer, E. (2015, April 27). Faculty in Canada may not need rules for using social media, observers say. Retrieved June 1, 2015 from http://www.universityaffairs.ca/news/news-article/faculty-in-canada-may-not-need-rules-for-using-social-media-observers-say/

Reddit. (n.d.). *I work in For-Profit Education. I hate myself for it. AMA.* [Online forum comment]. Retrieved June 1, 2014 from http://www.reddit.com/r/IAmA/comments/lkmdl/i_work_in_forprofit_education_i_hate_myself_for/

Reichmann, H., Wallach Scott, J., & Tiede, H. J. (2015). *Academic freedom and tenure: The University of Illinois at Urbana-Champaign.* American Association of University Professors report. Retrieved from http://www.aaup.org/file/UIUC%20Report_0.pdf

Rheingold, H. (2010). Attention, and other 21st century social media literacies. *EDUCAUSE Review, 45*(5), 14–24.

Rhoads, R. A., & Liu, A. (2009). Globalization, social movements, and the American university: Implications for research and practice. In J. C. Smart (Ed.), *Higher Education: Handbook of Theory and Research*, Vol. 24 (pp. 273–315). New York, NY: Springer.

Risam, R. (2014). A love letter to Twitter. [Web log post]. Retrieved August 10, 2014 from http://roopikarisam.com/2014/08/07/a-love-letter-to-twitter/

Rogers, A. (2001). Electronic journal usage at Ohio State University. *College & Research Libraries, 62*(1), 25–34.

Rogers, D. (2003). *Diffusion of innovations.* New York, NY: Free Press.

Ronson, J. (2015, February 12). How one stupid tweet blew up Justine Sacco's life. *The New York Times.* Retrieved August 13, 2015 from http://www.nytimes.com/2015/02/15/magazine/how-one-stupid-tweet-ruined-justine-saccos-life.html

Rothwell, P. M. & Martyn, C. N. (2000). Reproducibility of peer review in clinical neuroscience: Is agreement between reviewers any greater than would be expected by chance alone? *Brain, 123*, 1964–1969.

Rowe, K. (2010). Open review: *Shakespeare and new media.* Retrieved September 15, 2010 from http://mediacommons.futureofthebook.org/mcpress/ShakespeareQuarterly_NewMedia/

SAGE (2015). Authors – How to help readers find your article online. Retrieved February 23, 2015 from http://www.sagepub.com/authors/journal/discoverable.sp

Sajuria, J., VanHeerde-Hudson, J., Hudson, D., Dasandi, N., & Theocharis, Y. (2015). Tweeting alone? An analysis of bridging and bonding social capital in online networks. *American Politics Research, 43*(4), 708–738.

Scardamalia, M. & Bereiter, C. (2008). Pedagogical biases in educational technologies. *Educational Technology*, *48*(3), 3–11.

Schwier, R. (2012). The corrosive influence of competition, growth, and accountability on institutions of higher education. *Journal of Computing in Higher Education*, *24*(2), 96–103.

Selwyn, N. (2011). In praise of pessimism—the need for negativity in educational technology. *British Journal of Educational Technology*, *42*(5), 713–718.

Selwyn, N. & Grant, L. (2009). Researching the realities of social software use—an introduction. *Learning, Media and Technology*, *34*(2), 79–86.

Servon, L. J. (2002). *Bridging the digital divide: Technology, community, and public policy.* Maldeen, MA: Blackwell Publishing.

Shahjahan, R. A. (In press). Being "lazy" and slowing down: Toward decolonizing time, our body, and pedagogy. *Educational Philosophy and Theory*.

Sidlauskas, B., Bernard, C., Bloom, D., Bronaugh, W., Clementson, M., & Vari, R. P. (2011). Ichthyologists hooked on Facebook. *Science*, *332*(6029), 537.

Siemens, G. (2005). Connectivism: A learning theory for the digital age. *Journal of Instructional Technology and Distance Learning*, *2*(1).

Siemens. G. (2006). *Knowing knowledge.* Vancouver, BC: Lulu Publishers.

Siemens, G. (2013). Neoliberalism and MOOCs: Amplifying nonsense [Web log post]. Retrieved June 10, 2014 from http://www.elearnspace.org/blog/2013/07/08/neoliberalism-and-moocs-amplifying-nonsense/

Siemens, G. & Matheos, K. (2010). Systemic changes in higher education. *In education: exploring our connected educational landscape*, *16*(1), 3–18.

Solnit, R. (2014). #YesAllWomen changes the story. *TomDispatch*. Retrieved June 1, 2015 from http://www.tomdispatch.com/blog/175850/tomgram%3A_rebecca_solnit,_%23yesallwomen_changes_the_story

Solomon, G., Allen, N., & Resta, O. (2003). *Toward digital equity: Bridging the divide in the nation.* Boston: Pearson Education Group.

Solum, L. B. (2006). Blogging and the transformation of legal scholarship. *Washington Law Review*, *84*, 1071–1088.

Stafford, T. & Bell, V. (2012). Brain network: social media and the cognitive scientist. *Trends in Cognitive Sciences*, *16*(10), 489–490.

Stewart, B. (2012, May). The problem with EdX. *Inside Higher Ed*. Retrieved August 13, 2015 from http://www.insidehighered.com/blogs/university-venus/problem-ed

Stewart, B. (2015a). In abundance: Networked participatory practices as scholarship. *International Review of Research in Open & Distributed Learning*, *16*(3). Retrieved from http://www.irrodl.org/index.php/irrodl/article/view/2158

Stewart, B. (2015b). Open to influence: What counts as academic influence in scholarly networked Twitter participation. *Learning, Media, and Technology*, *40*(3), 1–23.

Stewart, B. (In press). *Attention in networked scholarship: Twitter as a site of care and risk.*

Sugimoto, C., Hank, C., Bowman, T. & Pomerantz, J. (2015). Friend or faculty: Social networking sites, dual relationships, and context collapse in higher education. *First Monday*, *20*(3). Retrieved October 21, 2015 from http://firstmonday.org/article/view/5387/4409

Summers, J. (2014, May 25). Educators not satisfied with revised Kansas social media policy. Retrieved June 1, 2015 from http://www.npr.org/sections/ed/2014/05/25/315837245/educators-not-satisfied-with-revised-kansas-social-media-policy

Tate, V. D. (1947). From Binkley to Bush. *The American Archivist*, *10*(3), 249–257.

Tennyson, R. D. (1994). The big wrench vs. integrated approaches: The great media debate. *Educational Technology Research & Development, 42*(3), 15–28.

Thackray, L. (n.d.). PhD Chat Wiki. Retrieved March 19, 2015 from http://phdchat. pbworks.com/w/page/33280234/PhDChat

Thagard, P. (1997). Collaborative knowledge. *Noûs, 31*(2), 242–261.

Thelin, J. R. (2013). *The rising costs of higher education.* Santa Barbara, CA: ABC-CLIO.

Thelwall, M. (2009). Homophily in MySpace. *Journal of the American Society for Information Science and Technology, 60*(2), 219–231.

Tiku, N. & Newton, C. (2015, February 4). Twitter CEO: We suck at dealing with abuse. *The Verge.* Retrieved from http://www.theverge.com/2015/2/4/7982099/twitter-ceo-sent-memo-taking-personal-responsibility-for-the

Tufekci, Z. (2008). Grooming, gossip, Facebook, and MySpace. *Information, Communication & Society, 11*(4), 544–564.

Tufekci, Z. (2012). Social media's small, positive role in human relationships. *The Atlantic.* http://www.theatlantic.com/technology/archive/2012/04/social-medias-small-positive-role-in-human-relationships/256346/

Tufekci, Z. (2014). Big questions for social media big data: Representativeness, validity and other methodological pitfalls. *Proceedings of the Eight International AAAI Conference on Weblogs and Social Media.* Ann Arbor, MI. Retrieved May 1, 2015 from http://arxiv. org/abs/1403.7400

Unsworth, J. (2000). Scholarly primitives: What methods do humanities researchers have in common, and how might our tools reflect this? *Symposium on Humanities Computing: Formal Methods, Experimental Practice.* King's College, London. Retrieved April 19, 2011 from http://jefferson.village.virginia.edu/~jmu2m/Kings.5-00/primitives.html

Van Noorden, R. (2014). Online collaboration: Scientists and the social network. *Nature, 512*(7513), 126–129. Retrieved December 10, 2014 from http://www.nature.com/news/online-collaboration-scientists-and-the-social-network-1.15711?WT.mc_id= TWT_NatureNews

Veletsianos, G. (2012). Higher education scholars' participation and practices on Twitter. *Journal of Computer Assisted Learning, 28*(4), 336–349.

Veletsianos, G. (2013). Open practices and identity: Evidence from researchers and educators' social media participation. *British Journal of Educational Technology, 44*(3), 639–651.

Veletsianos, G. & Kimmons, R. (2012a). Assumptions and challenges of open scholarship. *The International Review of Research in Open and Distance Learning, 13*(4), 166–189.

Veletsianos, G. & Kimmons, R. (2012b). Networked participatory scholarship: Emergent techno-cultural pressures toward open and digital scholarship in online networks. *Computers & Education, 58*(2), 766–774.

Veletsianos, G. & Kimmons, R. (2013). Scholars and faculty members' lived experiences in online social networks. *The Internet and Higher Education, 16*(1), 43–50.

Veletsianos, G. & Kimmons, R. (2015). Scholars in the digital age: Education scholars on Twitter. Manuscript submitted for publication.

Veletsianos, G., Kimmons, R., & French, K. (2013). Instructor experiences with a social networking site in a higher education setting: Expectations, frustrations, appropriation, and compartmentalization. *Educational Technology, Research and Development, 61*(2), 255–278.

Vygotsky, L. (1978). *Mind in Society.* London, UK: Harvard University Press.

Wakefield, J. (2013). President Stephen Toope talks money, MOOCs and bad reviews in annual State of UBC interview. *Ubyssey.* Retrieved May 30, 2015 from http://ubyssey. ca/features/toope/

Walker, J. (2006) Blogging from inside the ivory tower. In A. Bruns & J. Jacobs (Eds.), *Uses of Blogs* (127–138). New York, NY: Peter Lang.

Watters, A. (2014, October 17). Hack Education Weekly News: Yes, #Gamergate is an Ed-Tech Issue. Retrieved October 20, 2014 from http://hackeducation.com/2014/10/17/hack-education-weekly-news-10-17-2014/

West, R. E. & Rich, P. J. (2012). Rigor, impact and prestige: A proposed framework for evaluating scholarly publications. *Innovative Higher Education, 37*(5), 359–371.

Wesely, P. M. (2013). Investigating the community of practice of world language educators on Twitter. *Journal of Teacher Education, 64*(4), 305–318.

Weller, M. (2011). *The digital scholar: How technology is changing academic practice.* London: Bloomsbury Academic.

White, D. & LeCornu, A. (2011). Visitors and residents: A new typology for online engagement. *First Monday, 16*(9). Retrieved May 3, 2015 from http://firstmonday.org/ojs/index.php/fm/article/view/3171/3049

Whitworth, A. & Benson, A. (2010). Learning, design, and emergence: Two case studies of Moodle in distance education. In G. Veletsianos (Ed.), *Emerging technologies in distance education* (pp. 195–213). Edmonton, AB: Athabasca University Press.

Wikipedia. (2015). In *Wikipedia*, the free encyclopedia. Retrieved from http://en.wikipedia.org/wiki/Wikipedia

Wiley, D. (n.d.). Defining the "open" in open content. Retrieved March 19, 2015 from http://www.opencontent.org/definition/

YesAllWomen (n.d.). In *Wikipedia*, the free encyclopedia. Retrieved May 18, 2015 from http://en.wikipedia.org/wiki/YesAllWomen

Zawacki-Richter, O., Anderson, T., & Tuncay, N. (2010). The growing impact of open access distance education journals: A bibliometric analysis. *The Journal Of Distance Education / Revue De L'Éducation à Distance, 24*(3).

Ziker, J. P., Wintermote, A., Nolin, D., Demps, K., Genuchi, M., & Meinhardt, K. (2014). Time distribution of faculty workload at Boise State University. Retrieved May 20, 2015 from http://scholarworks.boisestate.edu/cgi/viewcontent.cgi?article=1022&context=sspa_14

INDEX